CONFRONTING
Casual
CHRISTIANITY

CONFRONTING
Casual
CHRISTIANITY

CHARLES F.
STANLEY

**BROADMAN
& HOLMAN
PUBLISHERS**

Nashville, Tennessee

ISBN: 0-8054-0193-8

Dewey Decimal Classification: 248.4
Subject Headings: CHRISTIAN LIFE // DISCIPLESHIP
Library of Congress Catalog Number: 85.7764
Printed in the United States of America

All Scripture quotations are from the
King James Version of the Bible.

Study questions written by Yvonne Burrage.

Library of Congress Cataloging-in-Publication Data

Stanley, Charles F.
   Confronting casual Christianity / Charles F. Stanley.
      p.   cm.
   ISBN 0-8054-0193-8
   1. Christian life—Baptist authors. I. Title.
BV4501.2.S7193 1985
248.2'5   85-7764
                                                           CIP

02 01 00 99 98   5 4 3 2 1

Dedicated to my grandfather, *Reverend George Washington Stanley*, whose godly life and courageous preaching of the gospel have been a continuing inspiration to my life.

Contents

Introduction:

CONFRONTING CASUAL CHRISTIANITY

Several years ago an "Apathy Club" was formed on a certain college campus. The officers of the club advertised a meeting of the membership. Not one soul showed up. Explanation: They were *too apathetic* to attend.

Perhaps that true happening causes us to chuckle. Too apathetic to attend! Yet, that attitude is not at all laughable when we consider the dead, dull blight which has descended like a pallor over countless Christians. The dictionary defines apathy as "lack of feeling or emotion; impassiveness; lack of interest or concern; indifference." Its first cousin is complacency which carries with it the idea of self-satisfaction and lack of concern. Whatever you call the condition, it saps the vitality of the body of Christ.

This pathetic condition is summed up in the expression, "I couldn't care less." In fact, many a believer is so apathetic and complacent that he will not even couch it in words—too indifferent and unconcerned to articulate his/her spiritual state. "I don't know" is their prevailing mood. "I don't know" often means "I don't care."

In my denomination, our over fifteen and a half million Southern Baptists together baptized only one person per 41.4 church members during 1996. Surely you would think that every Baptist could win one person a year to Christ Jesus. This is a lamentable tragedy.

> Our denomination, whether we live or die, and the lost of our people, whether they are saved or perish without Christ, is determined by whether we care or are filled with vast, abysmal indifference: "O that my head were waters . . . that I might weep day and night for the slain of the daughter of my people!" (Jer. 9:1). The compassionate heart that seeks after those who know not Christ as a living Savior is our present greatest need.[1]

The prophet Amos was devastated and sickened with the sins of Israel, the commissioned people of God. He ran the gamut of their sins—self-indulgence, violence, class hatred, indifference to human suffering, ostentatious religion, hatred of righteousness, insincerity, hypocrisy, superstition, filthy immorality, and more! And he had a "woe" to pronounce on the complacent:

> Woe to them that are at ease in Zion, and trust in the mountain of Samaria, which are named chief of the nations, to whom the house of Israel came! (6:1)

What is the overrriding lesson of that woe? It is precisely this—apathy and complacency are hydra-headed sins which are an affront to God Almighty. Believers sin far more against the Lord by what they fail to do rather than what they do. We grapple more with the sins of omission rather than commission.

The severest sin of Christians is a numbing lack of concern, an anesthetized attitude of "I don't care. I'm in the fold. Why should I concern myself? I have a fire insurance policy against hell."

One unknown Christian wrote:

> When Gideon was through thinning out his frightened and indifferent soldiers, he discovered that only one out of one hundred was brave and really meant business. I trust there is a better percentage of courageous and sincere people in our church membership today. However, it has been stated that "one fourth of the members of the average church could be dropped from the rolls and they would never know it happened, and the church would be no weaker as a consequence." The unorganized indifference within the ranks of the church members is far more destructive to the work of the Lord than all the organized forces of iniquity assailing from the outside.

My guess is that the percentage is closer to one half rather than one fourth. Is it a wonder that people are rushing headlong to perdition? While you read these lines, thousands are perishing, "dead in trespasses and sins." Apathy, complacency, indifference, spiritual drowsiness, and insensitivity are lulling the church of the Lord Jesus Christ to sleep.

One of the most poignant passages in God's Word is found in Matthew 26 (see also Mark 14, Luke 22). Jesus was approaching His betrayal by Judas and His arrest by ungodly authorities. Let us set the scene from Matthew's Gospel:

> Then cometh Jesus with them into a place called Gethsemane, and saith unto the disciples, Sit ye here while I go and pray yonder (v. 36).

Sometimes all Jesus asks of us is to sit and wait on Him. That was all in this instance. When He does make that request, He does rely on us to be alert and ready for His call. At this moment only a few of us are being called on to die in His behalf. All He asks of most believers is to watch and pray—to allow Him to live His life through them.

How insensitive and uncaring the disciples were. Jesus in the upper room, when He instituted the Memorial Supper, and en route to the Garden of Gethsemane had poured out His soul as an oblation before them. Yet, they did not seem to understand the agony and travail through which He was passing.

They were numbed with the novacaine of indifference. Imagine it. These were not His enemies, but His disciples, followers, and friends. Only one verse before, Peter had boasted:

> Though I should die with thee, yet will I not deny thee, Likewise also said all the disciples (v. 35).

Jesus, according to verse 37, "took with him Peter and the two sons of Zebedee [James and John], and began to be sorrowful and very heavy."

Our Lord recognized that He would become sin for us. Paul would later write: "For he hath made him to be sin for us; who knew no sin that we might be made the righteousness of God in him" (2 Cor. 5:21). In a matter of hours He would fulfil the role for which He entered the world. As Maxwell expressed it in a book title, Jesus was *Born Crucified.* Voluntarily the Lord would assume the heinous, horrid sins of the whole world—every sin, iniquity, and transgression in human history before that time, during that time, and until the end of the world! John the Baptist had prophetically announced, "Behold the Lamb of God, which taketh away the sin of the world" (John 1:29).

And Isaiah had peered down the tunnel of time and written about "a man of sorrows, and acquainted with grief" (53:3*b*). Isaiah received the revelation of the suffering servant who would die on the cross:

> Surely he hath borne our griefs, and carried our sorrows: yet we did esteem him stricken, smitten of God, and afflicted. But he was wounded for our transgressions, he was bruised for our iniquities: the chastisement of our peace was upon him; and with his stripes we are healed. All we like sheep have gone astray; we have turned every one to his own way; and the Lord hath laid on him the iniquity of us all (53:4-6).

That pulpit giant, the late Robert G. Lee, inquired: "Made sin—What does it mean?" He eloquently answered:

It means that God dealt with Him as He must deal with sin—in severe and unrelenting judgment!

It means that God sentenced sin, ordered sin to execution in the person and death of His Son. Jesus has made up before God for all we failed to do and be. Jesus takes all our sin and sins upon himself and bestows all his righteousness upon us. Jesus took sin's place on the cross! Took the guilty culprit's place there! Took my place there!

It means that He, the perfectly Righteous One, was made sin that we, the unrighteous ones, might be made righteous. For God meted out to Jesus the full measure of punishment sin deserves. . . . He who was righteous was judged before God as unrighteous that we who are unrighteous should be judged before God as righteous! . . .

But! To speak of Jesus' suffering as intense physical torture only is a species of spiritual stupidity and intellectual clownishness. Because of the depths and vastness of sin's malignant nature, which caused feet of Deity to draw back with trembling, terms like bravery, courage, martyrdom, physical agony have no place because they contain no meaning big enough to fit His experience, when he "made his soul an offering for sin"—when He died a spiritual death as well as a physical death. He founded our joy in the deep bitterness of His own soul.[2]

Jesus was painfully aware of the ignominy which awaited Him. He had endeavored to share His profound grief with them: "My soul is exceedingly sorrowful, even unto death: tarry ye here, and watch with me" (v. 38). That was all He asked. He did not command them to arm themselves, even though a couple of them tried.

Peter more than likely hid his sword under his robe. Jesus did not request that they gird themselves up for death at the hands of the Roman soldiers and the Temple guards. Just wait in this spot and watch with Me. Keep a vigil while I pray.

Our Savior was being crushed as the shadow of the cross loomed over Him. The culmination of God's plan was barely around the corner. How can a conscientious Christian read this passage and not weep uncontrollably?

> And he went a little farther, and fell on his face, and prayed, saying, O my Father, if it be possible, let this cup pass from me: nevertheless not as I will, but as thou wilt (v. 39).

A parallel passage, Luke 22:39-46, records other vivid details of His Gethsemane ordeal.

> Being in agony he prayed more earnestly: and his sweat was as it were great drops of blood falling down to the ground (Luke 22:44).

So intense was His pre-crucifixion agony that blood gushed from the pores of His skin. And yet his complacent disciples snoozed.

> And he cometh unto the disciples, and findeth them asleep, and saith unto Peter, What, could ye not watch with me one hour? (Matt. 26:40).

And He is asking His churches today, "Could you not watch with Me this hour?" This hour when the venom of

Satan is injected into the veins of an ungodly world, this hour when the devil is having his heyday—and is now the prince of the power of the air and the ruler of spiritual darkness—this hour when countless churches are retreating, and really should be singing, "Like a mighty tortoise moves the church of God," instead of "Like a mighty army moves the church of God."

Because the disciples were not able to watch with Him, they bypassed a spiritual blessing of immense proportions. They would not share in His agony then—they would much later. Then they desired comfort and ease. They were so close to Him and yet so far away.

How loving and kind Jesus was and is. Instead of chiding them, and He could have done that justifiably, he simply reissued His orders: "Watch and pray, that ye enter not into temptation: the spirit is indeed willing, but the flesh is weak" (v. 41).

Yes, the Lord Jesus recognizes your weakness—that there are moments when you have impulses to obey and to please Him, but there is your struggle with the flesh, the "old man" who was struck a death blow when you were born again. The disciples fell prey not basically to fatigue or physical tiredness, but to the dumb canker of complacency.

In these pages I challenge you to confront the complacency of your individual life—and then the collective lives of our churches. From the Word of God I want to turn the penetrating searchlight of the Holy Spirit into the crevices of your spirit. Modern Christians are kin to the disciples in Gethsemane, not only because of a shared relationship with the Lord Jesus, but also because of the flesh.

Surely this time the disciples would pinch themselves and stay awake, but the Scripture proves otherwise:

> He went away the second time, and prayed, saying, O my Father, if this cup may not pass away from me, except I drink it, thy will be done (v. 42).

So . . .

> He came and found them asleep again: for their eyes were heavy (v. 43).

How often has Jesus checked on you and found you sleeping? Preacher. Church staff member. Sunday School teacher. Worker in the church. Member sitting on the pew.

It is hardly essential for me to repeat the outcome.

> And he left them, and went away again, and prayed the third time, saying the same words. Then cometh he to the disciples, and saith unto them, Sleep on now, and take your rest: behold, the hour is at hand, and the Son of man is betrayed into the hands of sinners. Rise, let us be going: behold, he is at hand that doth betray me (vv. 45-46).

Merely because the disciples "struck out" does not mean we have a license to fail our Lord today. You must recall that Jesus' followers later repented, and almost to a man they died excruciating deaths for Him. Only John the beloved apostle died a natural death. It is thought he lived to be ninety-five or one hundred, though he did suffer banishment to the prison Isle of Patmos.

Two thousand years of Christian history and the canon of Holy Scripture and the prayers of our Christian forefathers and the bloody trail of the church of the Lord Jesus have placed us in a position where we have absolutely no excuse.

Today we alibi, "But those disciples had everything going for them. They fellowshipped with the living Lord. They ministered with Him, following in His footsteps. They broke bread with Him. They were intimately acquainted with Him. We are so far removed from Him today." If that is our rationalization, we are fully as insensitive as they were, for

> Jesus Christ [is] the same yesterday, and to-day, and for ever (Heb. 13:8).

Jesus Christ is alive forevermore. He is resident within all those who have called on Him. Paul testified, "I am crucified with Christ: nevertheless I live; yet not I, but Christ liveth in me: and the life which I now live in the flesh I live by the faith of the Son of God, who loved me, and gave himself for me." He lives in you. Jesus Christ is just as much here as He was then, except we cannot touch Him physically.

The same power of the Holy Spirit is present. He empowers every born-again believer. This is the fulfillment of the Great Commission's promise, "Lo, I am with you alway, even unto the end of the world" (Matt. 28:20b).

The supernatural dynamic that moved the post-resurrection church in apostolic days has not been abrogated or withdrawn. Jesus declared:

> Verily, verily, I say unto you, He that believeth on me, the works that I do shall he do also; and greater works than these shall he do; because I go unto my Father (John 14:12).

And the Lord Jesus Christ has commissioned His church, and that commission is in force until "the end of the world," the consummation of the age. We are commanded to "teach all nations, baptizing them in the name of the Father, and of the Son, and of the Holy Ghost" (Matt. 28:19).

Nothing has changed except we are two millennia closer to the glorious coming of our Lord.

And neither has our propensity toward a casual, comfort-seeking brand of Christianity—a Christianity without the "cup" and the cross, a line-of-least-resistance faith.

In the Christian community there is an inordinate amount of posturing about the problem of indifference in the ranks. Yet, there is a shortage of remedies for that complacency. Will "the last trumpet" be the only instrument to awaken slumbering, groggy Christians? Is there a road away from the debilitating effects of casual Christianity?

In the following pages, aided and abetted by the

Spirit, I wish to confront head-on the complacent variety of Christian discipleship found in our churches. As antidotes to the poisons of apathy and complacency, I suggest two words: *commitment* and *obedience.*

Chapter 1, "Committed," defines the seriousness of commitment to Jesus Christ. Chapter 2, "The Call to Commitment," pivots around Moses' call to lead the nation of Israel out of bondage in Egypt. Daniel is the example of commitment in Chapter 3, "Motivation for Commitment," as his obedience to the Lord was weighed. Jonah, the petulant prophet, is the focus of Chapter 4, "Resistance to Commitment." Abraham's willingness to sacrifice Isaac is the central scene of Chapter 5, "Commitment on Trial." The healing of Naaman the leper is the key event of Chapter 6, "The Rewards of Obedience." Finally, the Epilogue is a recap and summation of the previous chapters.

Through the vehicle of this book—but most of all through The Book, the Word of God—may you confront your own spiritual condition even as I grapple with mine. May the truths of The Book, which is my major resource here, open our eyes that we may see, free our minds that we may think on Him, loosen our tongues to sing His praises and witness for Him, activate our feet to "go" for Him, and energize our entire being to confront casual Christianity in our lives and in those of our brothers and sisters in Christ!

Notes

1. W. A. Criswell, *With a Bible in My Hand* (Nashville: Broadman Press, 1978), p. 190.

2. Robert G. Lee, *Grapes from Gospel Vines* (Nashville: Broadman Press, 1976), pp. 21-22.

C H A P T E R 1

Committed

Romans 12:1-2

I beseech you therefore, brethren, by the mercies of God, that ye present your bodies a living sacrifice, holy, acceptable unto God, which is your reasonable service. And be not conformed to this world: but be ye transformed by the renewing of your mind, that ye may prove what is that good, and acceptable, and perfect will of God.

Why do you suppose there are close to one hundred million church members in America, and yet they are not making the moral and spiritual impact they should?

Why is it that on Sunday morning thousands of churches have more empty pews than full?

How do you and I account for the fact that on most main streets in America the church doors are open on Sunday morning, but on Sunday night multitudes of churches have no services or only an activity going on in the corner?

The Bible is the revelation of God to us. This is His inerrant Word, His personal message to us. Why is it so few know so little about it?

If God is really a prayer-answering God, and if He meant for us to ask, seek, and knock (see Luke 11:9-10), why is there so little genuine praying going on?

If you and I believe there is a heaven and a hell, why do we keep so quiet about the gospel of Jesus Christ? If "there is none other name under heaven given among men, whereby we must be saved," then why are we not sharing the message of His amazing grace? Why are we keeping the Good News to ourselves?

Why are so many pastors having to beg and plead for members to give through the church budget, wringing their hands and fearful they are not going to pay their bills, and with their churches head over heels in debt, owing everybody and his brother but the Lord?

There is a common answer to all of those questions—and it is tragically simple.

And the answer is:

> God's people, most of them, have made a decision about Jesus . . . but have never made a commitment to Him.

There is a vast difference between a decision to do something and a commitment to the Person.

Many people who are saved and many who are church members were convicted by the Holy Spirit, and they made these kinds of decisions:

"I don't want to go to hell."

"I want to go to heaven when I die."

"I'm sick and tired of this mess I'm in."

"I'm upset about the way I've been living."

"I want help, and I want a new life."

They made a decision to receive the Lord Jesus Christ as their Savior. They did not want to spend eternity in hell. They wanted to enter heaven; they wanted to leave that disgusting old life. They desired God's forgiveness, so they received it. They wanted His pardon and His approval. They yearned for assurance, and they accepted it. Make no mistake about it. They invited Jesus Christ into their lives, and that was a definite decision.

In the lives of most professing Christians, there are not many healthy life signs. Why? I repeat: *because no one explained to them the difference between a decision to do something and a commitment to the Person, Jesus Christ.*

Why are at least fifty percent of all marriages either on the rocks or headed for them? Why are so many people divorcing? Why are so many simply living with each other without the benefit of wedding vows? Why are people "running around" and being unfaithful?

Every person who married made a decision. They

stood before an official of the church or of the state, and the officiant asked them several questions. The bride and groom answered:

> "Yes, I will take him/her to be my lawful wedded husband/wife."

They spoke vows to each other. And then they made a decision.

> "I will live with him/her 'til death do us part."

A decision was involved. Then the preacher or justice of the peace declared to them, in one form or fashion:

> "On the basis of those vows, and as you have joined hands and exchanged rings, I pronounce you husband and wife."

And if a pastor was in charge, more than likely he intoned:

> "In the name of the Father and the Son and the Holy Spirit, those whom God hath joined together, let not man put asunder."

They made a decision; they kissed each other; they walked out together; and they have been living ever since . . . not necessarily "happily ever after" and not necessarily together! But when a couple marries, and they truly make a commitment to each other, that is a different matter.

To explain the meaning of commitment, I refer to certain New Testament words from the original which best describe commitment. Put them all together, and they have different nuances of the same meaning.

Ten different Greek words are translated *commitment* in the New Testament. There are, however, two I mention here as most accurately describing Christian commitment: *paratithemi* and *pisteuō*.

In 1 Peter 4:19 is the statement, "Wherefore, let them that suffer according to the will of God commit [lay down, *paratithesthosan*] their souls before him in welldoing as unto a faithful creator." Here the word means to lay down something for Christ.

In John 2:24 is the phrase, "But Jesus did not commit [*episteusan*] himself unto them because he knew all men." This word is normally translated "to have faith in" or "to believe in." Here it means that Jesus was not willing to entrust Himself to them.

According to the Word of God, to make a commitment means to turn something over to someone.

It implies *committing* it to them, *yielding* to them, *surrendering* to them, *abandoning* it to them, *entrusting* it to them, and *placing it at their disposal.* When a person makes a commitment in the New Testament, God knows nothing of this hemming and hawing: "Yes, I want to receive You as my personal Savior. Thank you very much. Now, I'll take care of things until You call me home to heaven. But for right now, I'll just sort of do my thing."

Sadly, that is the decision of many. When a man or a woman makes a commitment in marriage, they are testifying to the whole world, "I abandon myself. I turn my back on all others. And I do this until death alone shall part us."

In essence, a woman is admitting, "I am entrusting my life to you as my husband, even changing my name."

A man is vowing, "I am willing to surrender myself, to give myself to you as your husband—to take care of you and provide for you until death parts us. And that is my commitment!"

The divorce courts would have to close down, and many lawyers majoring in divorce cases would go out of business if people truly made a commitment in marriage and not merely a decision. And if the majority of Christians had made a genuine, intelligent, unreserved commitment to Jesus Christ, the church houses would not hold the people trying to cram and jam into them.

Now what is involved in making a commitment? Christian, perhaps you have been a follower of Jesus for twenty, thirty, forty, or more years, but I want to ask you:

> Since you were saved, has there been a time in your life when you consciously committed all of your life to Jesus Christ—without hesitation, without reservation, without bargaining with God?

I firmly believe that there is no such thing as "partial commitment." No one can be "sort of committed." You are either committed or not committed. But I want to make a pertinent point—there is a difference between what one would try to call partial commitment and degrees of commitment. Let me illustrate. Maybe you were saved twelve, twenty, twenty-five years ago. And you did not understand much about going deeper in the Christian life. Yet, you promised the Lord, "Lord, I'm trusting you as my Savior. I give you my whole life." You made a commitment, although you did not understand all that was involved, and who does when they are first saved?

In a short time, God began to zero in on your life and commanded you, convicting you that He wanted this or that for your life. He was in the process of working out His will for you—and so you made another commitment. And another. And another. Twenty years of age, thirty years, forty, fifty, sixty, seventy, eighty, even ninety, you will still be making commitments to your Lord.

As God works in your life and mine, He *brings us to a deeper level of commitment*. At this point in my life, I may be totally committed to Him. But God may make a request of me at six o'clock tomorrow morning when I am asking Him to give me direction for the day. "Charles, I want this for your life."

But suppose I answer, "Lord, hold it right there. Wait a minute. I may have been committed on Sunday, but I'm not committed on Monday." By my very protest I would have become less than totally committed.

I repeat: there is no such thing as partial commitment. When the pilot of a giant airliner is speeding down the runway, there is a certain point where he cannot decide to remain on the ground. When he crosses that line, he is committed to the air, or either the plane crashes disastrously to the ground. That pilot cannot change his mind when the plane is two-thirds of the way down the runway.

Unfortunately, our churches are filled with members who "have never left the ground." They have been sitting there for years and years gunning their engines. "Vrooomm. Vrooomm. Vrooomm." They are always "prepping," getting ready. They are going to get busy. They have been planning on it, meaning to, wanting to, trying to, going to, aiming to, hoping to. But, tragedy of tragedies, they have never left the ground!

That grieves the heart of God Almighty: God has blessed you, equipped you, gifted you. You have good health, material possessions, plenty to keep you alive and kicking. You have sunshine. You have rain. You have a free country. You can travel anywhere you please, and you are luxuriating in the blessings of the Lord. It breaks His heart to see you sitting on the runway and revving up your engines all these years. You never have left the ground!

Being committed to Jesus Christ is deadly, serious business. It is a dangerous plight for you to remain on the ground, for if you do the Lord could permanently ground you. "For whom the Lord loveth he chasteneth, and scourgeth every son whom he receiveth" (Heb. 12:6). If He chastised us as we deserved, we could never keep up with the funerals.

Oftentimes God calls on us and we alibi, "Well, Lord, I want to thank You for giving me this opportunity, but here's what I'm going to do. I don't think that's what I ought to do, so what I'm going to do is this, and I'm going to do this so well."

And then, bullheaded and stubborn, we gear up, strive, work, and seek to excel outside of God's will. And we may impress the people who watch our jousting. What the world does not understand is where we belong and where we ought to be is over here where God instructed us to be. Sadly, many people are smart enough, wise enough, and shrewd enough to con people into believing that being outside of God's will is fully as good as being in it. Many of God's preachers are in that category. They have entered another profession and no longer preach, excusing themselves with, "I can serve the Lord just as well over here." Now, many godly men are bivocational. I am talking here about the man who quits ministering and preaching when it is clear God wants him to remain steadfast.

One man I know accepted the call to the mission field—to serve the Lord anywhere, but his wife did not agree. "No, I'm not going to the mission field." That man had to make a choice—to go or not to go.

He decided not to go. He rationalized, manipulated,

and finagled God's Word and his own feelings until he finally convinced himself that he should not go. His ministry grew by leaps and bounds. "Everything was coming up roses." All of a sudden, God removed him from the scene.

God is so good, so gracious, so kind, so longsuffering—and I am afraid that if the real truth were known, we play around with God far more than we realize.

I could fill up this book with instances of those who have tried to compromise their convictions and calling. I can think of another fellow whom God called to a specific task. The man came up with more arguments than a Philadelphia lawyer. He bowed his neck and answered God, "No, I'm not going to do that." He had his own plans. He pulled the same trick.

Instead of letting God decide on his ministry, the man tried to manufacture his own. Never in my life have I seen such a mammoth effort put forth to make a ministry (outside the will of God) succeed in the name of God. With no warning at all, God removed that man in a situation that was totally ironic. How could that have happened? God took him on.

You are asking, "Are you saying that if we don't do God's will, God's going to kill us?" No, but when He calls you to do certain things important to Him, and you stubbornly refuse to do them, He surely can remove you from the scene, either by death or inability to function and perform. Friend, *commitment to Jesus Christ is serious business.*

If you refuse to obey Him, God may not take your life, but you will never reach the maximum of your potential. You will never have the contentment, joy, and peace you might have experienced.

When you are "out of pocket" and not where the Lord wants you to be, you are never going to "get it together." You are going to trudge laboriously through life, missing God's best for you. Even to the Christian, life without commitment can be a drudge.

A central truth of commitment is that we no longer belong to ourselves. Paul asked:

> What? know ye not that your body is the temple of the Holy Ghost which is in you, which ye have of God, and ye are not your own? (1 Cor. 6:19).

The problem is that most people do not grasp the heavenly, eternal transaction that occurred when they were saved. Back to our text, Romans 12:1-2.

Verse 1 beseeches or urges the Romans to present themselves. It was on the basis of God's mercy toward them—"by the mercies of God."

Seize upon this truth: *commitment to Jesus Christ means the commitment of my total person.* When Paul refers to *bodies* here he is not merely referring to skin and bones, but to the total person.

Nearly all of us will meet folks who seem to have a huge sign written across their chests: "Reserved." Or maybe it is: "Keep Out" or "Don't Trespass." You can pick up the hint from their manner, their attitude, and their conversation. The message is rather clear: "Don't bother me about the details of living the Christian life. I'm saved. Just don't bother me about tithing and becoming involved and teaching Sunday School. I'm saved. I'm a Baptist," etc., etc., etc.

Friend, that is the antithesis of commitment. Commitment means that a person has deliberately, willfully chosen to give, to abandon his/her spirit, soul, and body to Almighty God through His Son Jesus Christ to the glory of God. And that implies a committed Christian has no right to put "Keep Out" or "Reserved" signs on his life.

Then, Paul went on to write: "I beseech you therefore, brethren, by the mercies of God, that ye *present your bodies* a living sacrifice." The word translated "present" here is the Greek technical word used for offering a sacrifice.

When a person offered a sacrifice during biblical times, and it was turned over to the priest, it was a presentation. The sacrifice was turned over, presented, relinquished, yielded. The person presenting the sacrificial lamb to the burning altar of sacrifice, to be consumed by fire to the glory of God, was giving up all claims to the animal. Commitment, then, is the personal, deliberate presentation of spirit, soul, and body to what? To God's use.

Commitment means, "Lord, I am climbing on that altar as though I were that lamb. Here I am." It means I present myself to Jesus Christ; I consciously lay myself on the altar.

When the lamb of sacrifice was presented—its throat slit and its blood drained—it was burnt on the altar. Then, it was too late to request its return.

What has happened to most believers? Early in their experience they were on the altar a few weeks or months, but they began to look around and, with the aid of the devil, thought about "all they were missing." So, with red face, they crawled off of the altar and started "playing footsie" with the world. They were saved but no longer a sacrifice. The altar was emptied. At one time they were abandoned to Him, yielded to Him, surrendered to Him, given to Him.

"Lord, what wilt thou have me to do? (Acts 9:6a).

"Here am I; send me" (Isa. 6:8c).

"Have Thine own way, Lord."

"Wherever He leads, I'll go."

Once those commitments were sweet, but now they may have deserted the altar.

Paul continues: "a living sacrifice, holy. . ." The word holy is *hagios* in the Greek, meaning that which has been deliberately separated unto God for His service.

At this juncture let me ask, How many of you readers have completely surrendered and yielded yourselves to

God for whatever He wants to do to you, in you, through you, and by you? You are committed to Him "with no strings attached." All of the "Reserved," "No Trespassing," and "Private Property" signs are gone. Have you prayed, "Lord, whatever You want, whenever You want it, however You want it, I am available. Here am I"?

This was the plea of Paul's heart as he realized what Christ requires of us. *Hagios* also means set apart for a particular use. It implies availability and usability. I ask you with all the fervor of my being, How many of you can honestly testify, "I am available to God for whatever He wants me to do in my life. There are no small-print clauses. I have burnt all of my bridges behind me. I really want to know what the Lord would have me do"?

We are prone to declare all of the above but then add, "But, Lord." And then tack on, "If I could just . . . I'm just . . . If only . . ."

For our remembrance I remind you that commitment is putting one's whole spirit, soul, and body at God's disposal on the altar, ready for His use anytime, any-place, anywhere, under any circumstances.

The opposing forces you and I feel are primarily *the lure of the world* and *the love of convenience*. We are not committed because we flirt with the snares of the evil world system. Commitment means separation from the world (see 2 Cor. 6:17-18). Commitment means leaving the lust of the flesh and the lust of the eyes and the pride of life behind us (see 1 John 2:15-17).

And how we love comfort and convenience! It is easy to curl up at home with the TV. After all, you've worked hard all day. You have so little time for yourself and your family. Like Felix before Paul, you look for "a convenient season" (see Acts 24:25).

During World War II, when our nation was threatened with calamity, millions of Americans flocked to church and prayed perhaps as they have not since. Today will anything bring us to our knees? Yet, I believe if our security were threatened severely, many Americans would pack our churches. What will it take for us to become committed?

What amazes me is: in the light of God's goodness, we are not committed. Think back. Recall the convicting power of the Holy Spirit in your life, His wooing you to salvation. Then God began to motivate you to serve Him. He has given you Christian friends, the church, people to encourage you and nurture you—He has opened up the truths of His Word to you. He has sustained you through thick and thin, keeping you by His power. He has never deserted you, never failed you, never let you down. Your cup has literally run over, and you cannot possibly begin to describe all God has done for you.

Talk about being good! He has been good to all of us. Even though we have faced a few burdens, heartaches, and valleys, the blessings have outweighed them.

What more motivation do we need than the cross of Christ? How much more motivation do you and I need than God's outpouring of superabundant blessings day after day after day?

Have you ever quit struggling and honestly laid down your arms at the feet of Jesus? Maybe you would confess, "Lord Jesus, I am weak. I am frail. But God, as best I know how, I yield myself to you. I really want Your best. I want my life to count for You, whatever it takes. I want to be obedient, whether I always like it or not."

"Here is my life, Lord. I am willing to be used in a little way in a quiet place, where no one much will know me. I am also willing to be used in a big place, wherever You wish. It doesn't make any difference. I just give myself to You." Have you ever done that?

I had to reach that place in my life. When I was a junior high kid delivering newspapers in Danville, Virginia, I told God: "Lord, I want to be what You want me to be, if I never even leave this town. Make me what You want me to be."

My paper route was one long street, North Main. For five years I delivered papers twice every day, then once on Saturday and once on Sunday, and I went two or three years without missing a delivery except for sickness.

When God called me to my first church up in Fruitland, North Carolina, in the mountains, I promised the Lord I would stay there as long as He wanted me to. All that mattered was living obediently and honoring Him.

Now, I did not ask to be where I am. God could remove me in the twinkling of an eye, and He could do the same to you. If you wait for God to do "big stuff" in your life, you may be waiting until Jesus comes. He simply does not operate like that. He wants you to be willing to be hidden and unknown, unappreciated, unheralded, and unthanked—if necessary—in order to do what He wants you to do.

Many people want loads of praise, honor, and publicity so they can "start serving the Lord." Oh, no. God does not move like that. He wants us to have the spirit of a servant like Jesus Christ. He came not to be ministered unto, but to minister.

Has the lure of the world made you draw a circle about yourself and tell God, "Lord, this is as committed as I am going to be"?

Innumerable Christians have claimed, "Lord, I'll go anywhere you want me to go. You just name it, God, and I'll go there."

"Whatever you tell me to do, Lord Jesus, I'm willing to do it. Just give the word."

But they have deliberately confined themselves to a circle of personal convenience, and they have no intention of stepping out of their own self-made boundaries. That is not commitment.

Can you begin to imagine how God's great heart feels after all He has invested in you, even every drop of His Son's precious blood?

Yes, they want to serve God but within their own parameters. "Lord, I'll serve within easy driving distance of my parents" or "I'll accept the church which pays more bucks" or "I'll teach a class, but I won't be able to contact absentees or help visit prospects."

The fact is: life itself is not that convenient. It was not convenient for you mothers to serve as a taxi service for your kids and others all those years, but you did it so they could have a well-rounded life of school, music, sports, extracurricular and church activities. It was not convenient for many of you dads to make the sacrifices you did so your wives and children could have a decent life. Working faithfully and productively at the job was not always convenient. Many are the days you wanted to call in sick (and you were really sick), but you did not.

The Bible is not a book for our convenience. It speaks about commitment and sacrifice and going the second mile, leaving all to follow Jesus. It talks about putting on the armor of a soldier and "enduring hardness as a good soldier of Jesus Christ." Commitment is written across its pages from Genesis 1:1 through Revelation 22:21.

In our church I have at times asked our folks to sign a simple card of commmitment which states: "I am totally available to God and want to be obedient to Him by committing myself in service and ministry." And I have asked our members, "Are we asking you to do anything God hasn't already asked you to do?" "For we are created in Christ Jesus unto good works" (Eph. 2:10).

The time has come when convenience does not compute. If you are going to be obedient to God, you must determine to quit sitting on the runway and revving up your motors. You must determine to fly. As it were, you ought to affirm in your heart: "I have sat long enough. I have been gunning my engines for months or even years, and now, Lord, I am ready to fly. I am ready to be used of You."

First Corinthians 3 teaches that one of these days you and I as Christians are going to stand before God to give account of ourselves (see vv. 11-15).

Even as Christians, we cannot have the approval of the Lord by "doing our own thing," by seeking the line of least resistance. It is high time for us to put our entire lives where our profession has already been for months, for years, maybe even for decades. For the pilot on the runway, there is a definite point where he cannot decide to stop the flight or turn back without disastrous consequences. Commitment makes the difference.

If Christ Jesus is actually Lord of your life, I do not believe you can sit without serving Him in one form or fashion. He has called us, He has saved us, He has equipped us, He has given us everything we have.

Jesus *died* for you. Right now He is asking you to *live* for Him. Someday, quite frankly, He may call on you to die for Him. I am not going to rule that out—but for the present He requests that you commit yourself, turn yourself over to Him, give of yourself, present yourself. Relinquish all claims to your life. Lay aside the easy road, the pathway of convenience . . . away with a bogus brand of Christianity that does not issue a clarion call for commitment.

He beseeches you by His mercies to present your

spirit, soul, and body to Him as a holy, acceptable, living sacrifice. That is your reasonable service—the least you can do. And let Him transform you instead of your being conformed to the lure of the world and the love of convenience. Then, and then only, will you be able to prove the good, and acceptable, and perfect will of the Heavenly Father.

Within your heart sing:

> Take my life, and let it be
> Consecrated, Lord, to Thee;
> Take my hands and let them move
> At the impulse of Thy love.
>
> Lord, I give my life to Thee,
> Thine forevermore to be.
> Lord, I give my life to Thee,
> Thine forevermore to be.
>
> —Frances Ridley Havergal

C H A P T E R 2

The Call to Commitment

Exodus 3:1-6,10-12

Moses presents one of the most persuasive lessons concerning commitment to God. God challenged him to a seemingly impossible commitment in his life.

God directed Moses in a manner which applies to all of us today. God is not satisfied with "just" saints. He wants us to live under the Lordship of Christ. Less than total surrender is rebellion toward God. You may camouflage it; paint it; sophisticate it; but if you are not living under the Lordship of Christ, you are in known rebellion toward God.

First, there is the background. Then we deal with four basic questions that every one of us must consider for ourselves.

Moses was forty years old when he viewed a fellow Hebrew being mistreated by an Egyptian, so Moses moved in and killed the abuser. At that moment he could have started a rebellion and released or redeemed Israel.

However, that was not God's plan because Moses was

not ready. For forty years Moses had been on "the backside of the desert" (the west side). The backside of the desert is an apropos example and a timely phraseology for where Moses was. Why? Because he had come from affluence, position, power, and prestige in Pharoah's household . . . to become a sheep herder.

Egyptians could not stand sheep herders. They wanted no part of them. Here he was, the man God had chosen, tending to sheep on the backside of the desert in Midian. Moses had settled down long before and married the priest of Midian's daughter.

It seemed like a normal day to Moses. He was going about his shepherding as usual, and God presented him with an unusual message.

> The angel of the Lord appeared unto him in a flame of fire out of the midst of a bush: and he looked, and, behold, the bush burned with fire, and the bush was not consumed. And Moses said, I will now turn aside, and see this great sight, why the bush is not burnt. And when the Lord saw that he turned aside to see, God called unto him out of the midst of the bush, and said, Moses, Moses. And he said, Here am I (Ex. 3:2-4).

Many times God speaks to you and me. One of the reasons we may not hear Him is that we are too caught up in doing our own business, our own "thing." Even when He tries to speak with us through a unique situation, we are in such a hurry we pass right on by. How significant that the Scripture states, "And when the Lord saw that he turned aside to see, God called unto him out

45

of the midst of the bush. . . ." Then Moses, as many others in the Bible answered, "Here am I."

God instructed him, "Draw not nigh hither: put off thy shoes from off thy feet, for the place whereon thou standest is holy ground" (v. 5). Then God began a conversation that would eventually lead Moses to make a lifetime commitment to Him.

In this particular passage God is calling Moses to commit himself as the leader, the statesman, the guide, the counselor, and the judge of Israel. Given to Moses was a tremendous responsibility, under God's authority, to rescue a people whom God would make into a nation through whom the Messiah would come. The Messiah would usher in the possibility of salvation for all mankind, and He would do it through the nation of Israel.

So, after an absence of forty years, Moses was being called of God back to Egypt, back to confront the Egyptian leadership from whom he had run out of fear. That was seemingly an impossible assignment. It was "Mission Impossible." He would direct three million rebellious Israelites through a barren desert, virtually without food and water, to a Promised Land which He had already ordained. How could God expect anyone to do that?

The Christians of this nation are abundantly supplied with many resources, spiritual and material, and yet we are making a pitiful showing in our influence and impact on society. There is one pressing reason: we are not committed to the God of this Book, and we are not committed to the Great Commission which the God of this Book has given to each and every one of us personally.

Now, why are we not committed?

To answer, we must first handle four questions. If you and I are going to be totally committed to Jesus Christ, we must respond to these urgent questions.

And the first question is this: *"Who is this God?"*

Who is this God Who is challenging you and me to live in submission to His divine authority? It is arresting to notice what God said to Moses at the outset. First of all, do not come any closer. "You are standing on holy ground."

Now consider verse 6:

Moreover he said, I am the God of thy father, the God of Abraham, the God of Isaac, and the God of Jacob. And Moses hid his face; for he was afraid to look upon God.

Immediately God grabbed his attention. Then God introduced Himself. God recognized how vital it was for Moses to know Him. One of the reasons why so many people are not committed is that they quite frankly do not know God. They sort of know *about* Him. Who is this God who requires final authority in your life and mine?

Four times in this passage God identifies Himself in the same manner. Verse 6—"I am the God of thy father, the God of Abraham, the God of Isaac, the God of Jacob. And Moses hid his face; for he was afraid to look upon God."

Verse 7—"And the Lord said, I have surely seen the affliction of thy people which are in Egypt, and have heard their cry by reason of their taskmasters; for I know their sorrows."

Verse 8—"And I am come down to deliver them out of the hand of the Egyptians, and to bring them up out of that land unto a good land and a large, unto a land flowing with milk and honey; unto the place of the Canaanites, and the Hittites, and the Amorites, and the Perizzites, and the Hivites, and the Jebusites."

Verse 9—"Now therefore, behold the cry of the children of Israel is come unto me: and I have also seen the oppression wherewith the Egyptians oppress them."

Having identified Himself, having surfaced the problem, and then having focused upon the dilemma, God directed Moses:

> Come now therefore, and I will send thee unto Pharaoh, that thou mayest bring forth my people the children of Israel out of Egypt. (v. 10).

Notice how Moses alibied. "And Moses said unto God, Who am I, that I should go unto Pharaoh, and that I should bring the children of Israel out of Egypt?" (v. 11)

Then in verse 13, "And Moses said unto God, Behold, when I come unto the children of Israel, and shall say unto them, The God of your fathers hath sent me unto you; and they shall say to me, What is his name? what shall I say unto them?"

How interesting that Moses would broach that idea. Why, these were God's people. He was and is the God of Abraham, Isaac, and Jacob. Why did Moses ask, "What shall I say unto them?" Because the people of God had fallen into idolatry and had begun to worship the pitiful false gods of Egypt.

So, if Moses had merely reported, "God has sent me," they would have asked, "Why, what's his name?" God was most specific here. Four times he identified Himself. God was emphatic in verse 14:

And God said unto Moses, I AM THAT I AM: and he said, Thus shalt thou say unto the children of Israel, I AM hath sent me unto you.

God left no stone unturned. Verse 15 reiterates in part verse 6. God is the God of your fathers, the God of Abraham, the God of Isaac, and the God of Jacob. "This is my name for ever, and this is my memorial to all generations." In verse 16 there is the reemphasis on the same—the God of your fathers and the God of Abraham and Isaac and Jacob.

Jehovah wanted to make it abundantly and unmistakably clear as to His identity. He wanted Moses to absorb the extreme import and value of His name.

Now verse 15 serves as an example. The word for God here is *Elohim,* the first name for Him in the Bible. In Genesis 1:1 it is used: "In the beginning God [Elohim] created the heaven and the earth." Elohim stands for infinite power and absolute faithfulness. Next notice the capitalized LORD. Actually it is printed in caps and small caps. L-O-R-D! The word was considered so sacred and holy that a devout Hebrew would not even attempt to pronounce it. In Hebrew books you will see it written as a tetragram—either as YHWH or JHWH—standing for Yahweh or Jehovah. The ancient Hebrew language had no vowels, only consonants (they were added later on).

So, God was stating: "Thus shalt thou say unto the children of Israel, The LORD (Yahweh) God (the Elohim) of your fathers, the Elohim of Abraham, the Elohim of Isaac, and the Elohim of Jacob, has sent me unto you. The everlasting and eternal God, the self-existent Creator of the universe, the Maker of all things, the Sovereign of His creation, the One Who is infinite in power and absolute in faithfulness—He is the One Who has sent me."

Why would the people of Israel be willing to follow a leader who had left them forty years before for the life of a shepherd? What kind of military experience would he have? What was his strategy for rescuing three million Hebrews? What would they do for food and water, equipment, and provisions? And who claimed they would ever be delivered anyhow? That is why it was exceedingly important for Moses to tell them the nature of the God Who sent him as deliverer and leader.

This is mentioned in another chapter, but emphasis is required here. Real commitment does not have a limit. In essence many Christians are telling God, "I'll give You only so much, but I'm not going beyond this. These

are my outer limits." They try to strike bargains with
God. He will let them do that, but misery and unhap-
piness will be the long-term results.

It is as though we have told the Lord, "Yes, Lord, I am
willing to be married to You as long as I can hide the
marriage license, so at any time I choose to be unfaithful, I'll do it."

When you committed yourself to Jesus Christ—and
maybe you were not instructed about it—you forfeited
your "rights." You had joined a new nation in the spiritual realm. You were born into a new family. You became related to the living God. Christ Jesus became
your life; then your life choices came under the absolute
authority of the Person of Jesus Christ.

Like the Hebrews in Egypt, we have lost track of Who
God is. He is not a grandfather figure sitting in a rocking
chair up in heaven, merely watching us play, and turning
a deaf ear to our language, closing his eyes and winking
at our sinfulness. God Almighty not only is our Giver of
life, He is life!

I ask you: Do you believe your God, the God you
worship, is the God of the Holy Scriptures? The God of
Abraham and Isaac and Jacob? Do you believe He is the
God Who sent Jesus Christ, the Messiah, through that
family?

If you believe all of the above, then what right do you
have to reserve any part of yourself from Him—your
possessions, your energy, your time? If He is the God of
the universe and your God, how can you rebel against

His authority over your life?

The second question we ought to ask is the same put forth by Moses. In verse 11, Moses asked God, *"Who am I?"* "Who am I that I should go to Pharaoh and bring the sons of Israel out of Egypt?"

God did not answer, "Look, Moses, you are one of them." He did answer in verse 12: "Certainly I will be with thee; and this shall be a token unto thee, that I have sent thee: When thou hast brought forth the people out of Egypt, ye shall serve God on this mountain."

In a very real sense, Moses could not know *who God was* until he knew *who Moses was.* God had to tell Moses who he was—and He has to do that with us. You will never grasp or understand who you are until you are able to identify yourself with the Person of Jesus Christ, with the God Who created you!

There are several emotions and circumstances which plague Americans. Two of these are emptiness and pur-poselessness. Many people feel they are nobody. They have no value or worth at all. That is why countless people abuse themselves with illicit sex, alcohol, and drugs. They have no idea who they are or who God is.

All that makes you and me somebody is our rela-tionship to the Lord Jesus Christ. Deep down inside, through the Holy Spirit, He affirms who we are. We are His sons and daughters if we have accepted Christ. He is our God. We are "accepted in the beloved."

Who are you? Answer that within your heart.

Some would reply, "I am a Christian, I am a believer, I

am a follower of the Lamb of God."

Others would answer, "I'm a doubter, I'm a skeptic, I'm an agnostic."

Still others, and they are few in number, would claim (and it is usually done in arrogance), "I'm an atheist. I don't believe in God. I don't believe in a Supreme Being."

If you have ever placed your trust in Jesus Christ for salvation, you are a redeemed child of the living God, having been redeemed by the blood of His Son, Jesus Christ, at Calvary—that is who you are. You are a sealed saint, sealed by the Holy Spirit unto the day He comes back for you, and indwelt by the Spirit, with your name written in the Lamb's book of life. You are a disciple, a learner, a follower of the Christ, whether you follow afar off in sin or whether you follow close up. You are a servant of the eternal God, whether you serve well or poorly. You are a soldier in the army of the Lord Jesus Christ, whether you are in the front lines or AWOL.

You have been forgiven of your sin; you have been redeemed by the grace of God; you have been justified, declared righteous, and God now looks upon you as though you had never sinned. You have been pardoned from your sins by His blood. You have been reconciled to God through His Son, Jesus Christ. You have been sanctified, and are being sanctified (set apart) unto God and for Him. You have been glorified as a child of God, a child of the King.

The Bible teaches us that God Himself has set you

and me apart for the future that in the ages to come, He will point to us as His children and announce to the heavenly host—the angels, the cherubim, the seraphim—"Look at the demonstration of my eternal grace—these are the beloved whom My Son's blood bought at Calvary!" *That is who we are!*

You see why no Christian has the right to live his own life and do his own thing. If the God of this Book is your God, He has the final authority over your life. We are servants of Jesus Christ, but He also calls us His friends. You and I are His sons and daughters living in submission and subjection to Him, in honor of Jesus Christ who is our very life. *That is who we are!*

If I know who I am, and if I know who God is, then my so-called rights in life have been subjugated to the Person of God in Jesus Christ—*Christos*. He is the Lord of my life. And whatever and whenever, I have no cause to bargain with Him or put up an argument.

If you and I are purchased possessions of God, then all that has our names on it belongs to that same God.

There is a third question which presses upon us. *To Whom do I belong?* How did God put this truth across to Moses? Moses naturally began to tell the Lord, "Now, Lord, wait a minute. Hold it. Stop right there. Don't call little ole me. Who am I? Why, I'm nothing." That is so natural! And it sounds so much like the "natural man" (1 Cor. 2:14). The reason all of us are so skilled with excuses is that we inherited this propensity from Adam and Eve. Imagine it—the first human beings and you would think that they had studied Excuses I and II in the college of life. Sad, but it was Lucifer who taught them.

So many times God calls us, challenges us, and we turn around and protest, "Lord, wait a minute. You've got the wrong person." What an insult to the Lord, since He is omniscient—He knows everything. He is not going to make a mistake when He calls. He realizes precisely what we can do through His power. He is not going to call you for something you cannot do aided and abetted by His supernatural power.

We are so prideful that we try to give instructions to the Lord, and, as it were, we tell Him, "Lord, you know *almost* everything, but You surely have goofed this time. I can't do that, and I'm not the right person for this task. Get somebody else." You may not couch it in those words, but that is your meaning when you question the leading of the Lord, when you rebel against His guidance, when you sidestep His clear calling.

If He is perfect (and we know He is), He simply makes no mistakes. If He is all-knowing, He makes no blunders.

To Whom did Moses belong?

Who brought Moses into the world? God. Who preserved him when Pharaoh was having those boy babies put to death or either left to die when they were born? God. Who sent the servant of Pharaoh's daughter out to the Nile, there to find baby Moses in the little basket his mother had woven from the reeds of the river? God. Who caused Pharaoh's daughter to love that baby who would become the deliverer? God.

God saw to it that Moses grew up healthy and strong in the very household of Pharaoh. God equipped him, gifted him, blessed him, and made him ready for the call He would issue, To whom did Moses belong? God first and foremost.

Then Moses alibied, "They won't listen to me. Whom shall I tell them sent me?"

Moses sounds like the church members of today when the nominating committee is searching for workers. "But I can't . . ." Moses is so contemporary.

> And Moses said unto the Lord, O my Lord, I am not eloquent, neither heretofore, nor since thou hast spoken unto thy servant: but I am slow of speech, and of a slow tongue (4:10).

How convenient. "I can't speak well. I'm slow of speech. I'm tongue-tied." Do you ever hear that toward time for the election of Sunday School workers? In other words, "You are calling me to be your spokesman, but You don't know what you're doing, Lord." That is weird! Moses acted as though God was not aware of his problems.

Then God answered him:

> And the Lord said unto him, Who hath made man's mouth? or who maketh the dumb, or deaf, or the seeing, or the blind? have not I the Lord? (v. 11).

Hey, Moses, didn't I make your mouth in the first place—your lips, your tongue, your voice box? Don't you think I have the foggiest notion of what I am doing?

Already God had spoken to Moses out of the burning bush. He had identified Himself over and over again. He had explained Moses' role in delivering the Israelites, and He had performed one wonder after another. What would it take to convince Moses that God knew precisely what He was doing?

Earlier in chapter 4, God taught Moses with the transformation of his rod or shepherd's staff. The Lord asked Moses all kinds of questions, and He is still doing that today. In 4:2 God asked, "What is that in thine hand?" Moses answered, "A rod." How often God has to deal with us as though we were little children, and many of us adult Christians *are* spiritual babes.

God then demonstrated His power by asking Moses to throw that rod on the ground. "And it became a serpent and Moses fled from before it" (v. 3b). Then God instructed Moses to pick it up by the tail, and it became a rod again (v. 4). Moses certainly was tongue-tied with that request, maybe because he was petrified about having to pick up a snake! In verse 5 God spelled it out: I have given this demonstration of My power "that they may believe that the Lord God of their fathers, the God of Abraham, the God of Isaac, and the God of Jacob, hath appeared unto thee."

Would you believe that Moses did not seem to be convinced? So God told Moses to put his hand in his bosom, inside his garment on his chest. When he did and withdrew it, his hand "was leprous as snow" (v. 6). Leprosy was considered a horrible curse in Bible days and even in modern times. In verse 7, God directed Moses to put it back into his bosom, and the hand came out healed.

Now do not start running down Moses for his lack of faith. We imitate him nearly every day. How many times has God gone to the limits merely to arrest our attention? Sometimes He has to come down on us hard because nothing else will seize our attention. And that is drastic. Why not listen from the beginning and avoid all of the stress and strain?

How often we have rationalized, we have reasoned, we have alibied when God has tried to call us. Our churches are full of people who polish up their cases before the Lord. "Now, Lord, I'll be a witness with my life. I'll win people to Jesus by my example." That is not enough—an example *and* a verbal witness are called for. "Lord, not me, I'll stay here at home. You don't want me as a missionary. Not me." "Lord, I'm not articulate. I can't preach. Why, I can't even do much in our discussion group." On and on these alibis continue, and our friends, our neighbors, our loved ones, and multiplied millions of people all over the world are going to hell because there is a shortage of committed witnesses.

To whom do you belong? It is that simple. If you are the purchased possession of the Lord Jesus Christ, you do not belong to yourself. You honestly have no choice other than to obey. God is your final authority.

> What? know ye not that your body is the temple of the Holy Ghost which is in you, which ye have of God, and ye are not your own? (1 Cor. 6:19).

You are not your own. You belong to Jesus Christ if you have received Him. We as parents ought to teach our children, "We are your parents, but you are the purchased possession of Jesus Christ. We are in your life to help you reach the point where God and you can develop a relationship with each other. We are your earthly parents, but you belong to God." "Sweetheart, you belong to God." "My darling husband, you belong to God." Everything you have or hope to have belongs to Him—your life, your breath, your blood, your flesh, your bones, your talents, your time, your energy.

And you ought to consider your Source—the King of kings and the Lord of lords, the Ruler of the universe, the Redeemer, the Savior. It is abysmal arrogance and pride to presume that you own anything. You are indebted to God for every breath, every drop of blood. To ignore God's ownership and rulership, and your consequent stewardship, is sinful pride—an assumption of arrogance.

You and I have no right to tell God what we will do, where we will go, what we will think, and what we will give. It is not fitting for a believer to draw boundaries around his life and assert, "I am willing to do anything and everything You want, O Lord, except this or that." If you are really committed to Christ as Lord, you will pray, "Lord, what are Your orders?"

A person genuinely committed to Jesus Christ will answer, YES, YES, YES to the call of the Lord—whether he always likes it or not, whether it is painful or not, whether it is hurtful or not, whether he will be appreciated and understood or not. It will be, "Lord Jesus, if that's your call and requirement, I'll answer YES."

Our final question is pivotal: *Why am I here?*

When I settle these four questions, then my commitment issue should be determined forever. Why am I here? Why was Moses there? We have detailed the special providences of God in his life: rescued as a baby, reared as "the son of Pharaoh's daughter," lifted to early prominence in Egypt, escaped to the backside of the Midianite desert where God prepared him, called of God out of the burning bush, instructed in who he was and Who God is and shall always be.

God sifted him, molded, and made him. Even though Moses may not have realized it, he was not marking time on the backside of the desert. God was preparing Him for one of the most herculean tasks in the history of civilization—the Exodus from Egypt, the deliverance of God's people from cruel, oppressive bondage. Moses would be despised in the eyes of the "sophisticated" Egyptians—why, a rough, dirty shepherd from that forsaken desert country. God had sanded Moses down, sculptured him, and pruned out his pride that had existed when he was the son of Pharaoh's daughter.

Do you ever wonder why you have those "dry spells" in your life when nothing seems to go right but nothing especially seems to go wrong? Malaise seems to set in with nothing notable going on, so you think. And you ask, "What's going on?" Maybe you are on the backside of the desert spiritually. Such a period puzzles you, even makes you wonder if God is through with you.

God is readying you for future service, if only you will trust in Him. God wants you humbled to the extent that you cry out, "Lord, not my will but thine be done. I'll do what You want me to do! I'll do anything, anytime, anywhere. You name it, Lord Jesus, and I'll do it. I'll answer, Yes, Yes, Yes!"

That is why he has you on the backside of the desert; that is a precious place to be if you want to be used of God. He will put you there sooner or later because that is your spiritual "basic training."

He spent forty years of his life in Egypt, another forty years in the desert, and he had forty left. Moses was eighty years of age when God called him to the monumental task of leading the children of Israel out of Egypt en route to the Promised Land.

Sometimes young people talk with me, and they want to take a shortcut to the land of service. They want the "big places" of service without paying the price, without laboring on the backside of the desert. Jesus prepared thirty years for a three-year ministry. Moses had spent eight decades preparing for his key ministry. You cannot rush God. His timetables are different from ours.

Many times senior citizens remark, "I'm 75 (or 65 or 85, etc.) years old, and I don't know why God is leaving me here." Never even think that God has a specific plan for leaving you here. Maybe it is to help win your sons and daughters, your grandsons and granddaughters to Jesus. Maybe it is to encourage others who feel useless and no count. A long time ago you should have discovered why God keeps you here.

If you are a teenager you ought to understand why you are here. If you are ten years old, your parents should already have taught you why you are here. Why are you here as a single? Why are you here as a married person? Why are you here at eight or eighteen or eighty?

If you do not know why you are here, Jesus Christ will never be Lord of your life until you understand why. Ask the average person, "Why are you here?" and he will reply, "I don't know. I just happened. My parents had me, and I had no choice about it. I'm here and I don't know what to do about it." No, it was not an accident. You didn't just happen. They can think of scores of inane reasons. "I'm here to have fun." "I'm here to enjoy life." "I'm here to suffer." "I'm here to squeeze everything out of life I can." "I'm here to live and die and then furnish fertilizer for the ground."

Why are you alive today? There is one main reason. I am going to assume that you believe the Bible, and that you believe at least intellectually in the God of Abraham, and of Isaac, and of Jacob, and that you believe Jesus Christ is the Messiah and Savior, and that there is only one God and that all other gods are false gods. The majority of Americans at least claim to believe all of the above—maybe not with the heart but with the head.

Why are you here, then? If all of the above truths are valid (and they are), and the reason you are here is to be rightly related to that God, then if your life is not an expression of that truth, you must make a course correction immediately. Four central Scriptures will help answer the question, "What is my purpose in life?"

> Let your light so shine before men, that they may see your good works, and glorify your Father which is in heaven (Matt. 5:16).

One primary reason we are here is to glorify God, and in so doing, move others to glorify Him. Now consider Romans 15:6:

> That ye may with one mind and the mouth glorify God, even the Father of our Lord Jesus Christ.

First of all, we glorify Him by what? Our works. Second, by our voices. Now let me emphasize 1 Corinthians 6:19-20:

> What? know ye not that your body is the temple of the Holy Spirit which is in you, which ye have of God, and ye are not your own? For ye are bought with a price: therefore glorify God in your body, and in your spirit, which are God's.

We are to glorify God with our works, with our voices, with our bodies, and with our spirits. Then we turn to 1 Peter 2:12:

> Having your conversation honest among the Gentiles: that, whereas they speak against you as evildoers, they

may by your good works, which they shall behold, glorify God in the day of visitation.

This truth is paramount—we are to glorify God with our manner of living, our life-style. This means we must live to reflect the Lord Jesus. Homer Rodeheaver wrote the hymn "Jesus Revealed in Me." He called Christ "the transforming Light." When He transforms us, and puts His light into us, we are to reflect Him. Such lives will cause others to desire this Light. They will want to accept, submit to, praise, worship, and live in obedience to God.

All right, if our purpose for being here is to glorify Almighty God, there is one more question: "What could possibly allow you to live your life as you please when that is totally foreign to the Word of God?"

He is calling many who read these words. If you are in the pastoral ministry, perhaps He is calling you to stay put. Or maybe He is calling you to move. If He is, He will open up the door. Some of you are being called to different ministries, but many of you are remonstrating with Him that you either will not go or cannot go. I beg of you not to argue with the Lord. Answer, as Isaiah did, "Lord, here am I, send me."

Have you ever surrendered to Him lock, stock, and barrel, keeping back nothing, withholding nothing? Why not "let go and let God have His way," like that old chorus expresses it?

When you trusted Jesus Christ as your personal Lord and Savior, in the moment you did that, the Bible promised that Jesus became your Life, your All, your Sustenance, your Being, your Anchor, your Rock, your Refuge, and infinitely more! He is your everything.

How can you withhold yourself from Him?

C H A P T E R 3

Motivation for Commitment

Daniel 1:1-7

Why do some people achieve so much and others so little? Is it because the achievers are more talented than those non-achievers? Not necessarily.

Why is it that some people are excited and enthusiastic about what they are doing and energized to do well? At the same time, others with the same responsibility seem to be lackadaisical about the whole idea and have virtually no enthusiasm.

And why is it that two people can work side by side at the same occupation, and one is productive and the other not nearly as productive? One is charged up and the other is not.

And how can two children from the same family be so vastly different? One makes As and Bs and the other brings home Ds, Es, and Fs. Why?

What accounts for the difference? Two people can sit on the same church pew and listen to the same message. One can be thrilled about the Lord, desirous of pleasing Him, and applying spiritual truths. The other is blasé about it and never seems to make an application, never makes a note, never carries a Bible. The person is just there, and sometimes it is hard to figure why.

The difference is dreadfully simple—*motivation*. One person is motivated and the other is not. One is turned on and the other is not.

Motivation is the drive within us. It is that something within us which moves us, stirs us, punches our buttons, gets us moving. Different factors, of course, motivate different people. For example, some people are highly motivated by the approval of others or highly motivated by a sense of position or prominence. Others are motivated by more money; others by their appearance; others by unusual stimuli.

Let me ask, though, what motivates the people of God? What motivates you in your commitment to Jesus Christ? If commitment is the willful surrender on my part to Jesus Christ as Lord, what is required in order to motivate me to fulfill my Christian commitment?

If you are saved, you made a commitment to Jesus Christ. You promised Him, in essence, "Lord, from this point on in my life, this is what I am going to do. I am going to do this, and I am not going to do the other."

What motivates you to fulfill your commitment and follow through on it? In the life of Daniel, certain incidents served as specific motivators of his commitment.

We often express it simplistically, "Well, you know, if you love the Lord Jesus Christ, that ought to be motivation enough." True, but for many professing Christians that does not seem to be enough, sad to say. God uses many forms of motivation, and we are motivated by different factors.

The backdrop of the Book of Daniel was the invasion of Judah by cruel, despotic Nebuchadnezzar, the king of Babylon. He carried away King Jehoiakim, spoils from the Temple, and splendid young men of Judah,

> Children in whom was no blemish, but well favoured, and skilful in all wisdom, and cunning in knowledge, and understanding science, and such as had ability in them to stand in the king's palace, and whom they might teach the learning and the tongue of the Chaldeans.
>
> And the king appointed them a daily provision of the king's meat, and of the wine which he drank: so nourishing them three years, that at the end thereof they might stand before the king.
>
> Now among these were of the children of Judah, Daniel, Hananiah, Mishael, and Azariah.
>
> Unto whom the prince of the eunuchs gave names: for he gave unto Daniel the name of Belteshazzar; and to Hananiah, of Shadrach; and to Mishael, of Meshach; and to Azariah, of Abednego (Dan. 1:4-7).

The position in which Daniel and his three friends found themselves was not enviable. Nebuchadnezzar was a vicious, vile heathen, possessed with cruel barbarity. Nebuchadnezzar (sometimes Nebuchadrezzar) is often mentioned in Jeremiah, especially chapters 29, 34, 37, and 39. Nebuchadnezzar enjoyed pillaging and plundering. One of his favorite pastimes was killing a man's family while the fellow was forced to watch. He also often had his captives' eyes burned out (see Jer. 39:47) or had his prisoners boiled over a hot fire.

Daniel and his Hebrew friends were at the complete mercy of this Babylonian fiend. At any moment he could have had them tortured and then killed.

So, immediately these young men were faced with the royal command to transgress the Hebrew dietary and worship laws. Look at Exodus 34:14-15:

> For thou shalt worship no other god: for the Lord, whose name is Jealous, is a jealous God:
> Lest thou make a covenant with the inhabitants of the land, and they go a whoring after their gods, and do sacrifice unto their gods, and one call thee, and thou eat of his sacrifice.

The word jealous does not mean jealousy as we think of it among courting couples or husbands and wives today. It implies that He wants us to worship Him because it is for our good that we worship Him and Him only. In other words, He has the right to expect complete and undivided service and worship from us.

Daniel and his friends were keenly aware that the food and drink offered to them were dedicated to the false gods of Babylon. How, then, could they possibly survive and still live holy lives, refusing to defile themselves physically or spiritually? How could they remain true to Jehovah God and at the same time live in Babylon? You see, God had a reason for sparing them when so many of their kinfolks were wiped out by the

Babylonian invaders. Now they were in a strange land, a pagan society. So, two alternatives were offered them. They could have protested in this manner: "Well, we're just not going to do what you ask. We believe in Jehovah God. You can do whatever you like to us, but we are not going to follow your instructions."

But God gave unusual wisdom to Daniel and his friends as they responded wisely. Look at verse 8;

> But Daniel purposed in his heart that he would not defile himself with the king's meat nor with the wine which he drank: therefore he requested of the prince of the eunuchs that he might not defile himself.

The first motivation when it comes to obeying God and carrying out our commitment to Him is right here. You and I have made certain commitments to God. You have committed yourselves to trust Him as Savior, and since then you no doubt have committed yourself to Him again and again. You have yielded yourself to live in submission to Jesus Christ. That is, to live under the authority of His Lordship. You have affirmed, "Lord, You are the Supreme Head of my life. I acknowledge that, and I choose to be obedient to You."

What, then, should motivate us to carry out that commitment and to fulfill it, being obedient to Him?

First of all, inscribe *devotion* on the tables of your mind. Express your simple, personal, loving devotion to the Lord Jesus Christ. One primary reason Daniel would not defile himself was that very devotion.

To express devotion to God implies that you honor

Him as the only true God, that you recognize Him as the only One, that you worship Him as the only One, that you are loyal to Him and to Him alone as your God, and that you affirm your deepest love toward Him.

Now let me pose a question:

What governs whether or not you live committed to God?

Do you watch to see which way your friends are going? Do you sit on the fence and fall off on the popular side? Or is your devotion to Christ like an anchor that keeps the soul, an anchor that causes you to remain steadfast and true because of your loving devotion, motivated by your thanksgiving and praise for His saving and keeping you as one of His own?

How deep is your love for God? How can you measure it? The next time you are tempted to follow along with the world, your response to that temptation will divulge to you the degree to which you are devoted to the Person of the true and living God.

Daniel had determined within his being, the inmost depths of his heart, not to violate the wishes of his God. When he was challenged to violate the very precepts his parents had taught him, he refused to compromise. He made up his mind to obey God.

Have you ever made this sort of commitment? "Lord, through Your Son Jesus Christ, by the power of the Holy Spirit that indwells me, I shall obey You, regardless of the consequences."

Daniel followed through on his commitment, motivated by loving devotion to God Almighty. What have you decided to do?

There is a second motivation I want you to view. His motivation was also based on *clear direction*. Meditate on that. Daniel could have decided to say, "I'm not going to do what you are asking," but more than likely he and his friends would have been executed within a matter of hours.

When Daniel and his companions began to pray, God gave them an alternative to dogmatically violating the king's command, which could have cost them their lives. God had placed them there for a reason, and He gave them an alternate approach. They would humbly address Ashpenaz, the king's master, and ask a fair concession: "Allow us to drink water and eat vegetables for ten days while the others are drinking wine and eating meat. Then check us out and decide whether this diet was worthwhile. All we ask is a ten-day trial period. Then you be the judge. See if we don't look as well or even better than those on wine and meat."

This relates to us where we are. Whenever you are tempted to violate your conscience and the leading of the Holy Spirit, when you are challenged to violate God's plan and purpose for your life, do not try to be a big, brave martyr. You may end up being one, but do not make that your first choice.

You make your first choice to seek the mind of God

and ask, "Lord, is there an alternative? I am not going to violate Your will. Is there a way I can be submissive to those in authority over me, and at the same time not violate my conscience as it is controlled by the Spirit?"

Daniel was motivated by *clear direction.* Sometimes God makes it crystal-clear, but we do not want to accept the clarity of His leading. When God gives us a clear direction, one that is unmistakably understandable, it is a definite motivating factor. That is why a life of prayer, meditation, and searching the Word of God is pivotal. Most Christians have no clear direction because they are drifting and lazy.

Make time for communing with the Lord, feasting on His Word, and listening for His "still small voice." When you are assured that you have the mind of the Lord, it is amazing how motivated you will become. You will even be willing to "take risks" in the eyes of the world, but it's never a risk on your part to be obedient to God!

I can vividly remember when the Lord was challenging me to come here to First Baptist Church of Atlanta. I was in a revival meeting at Alexandria, Virginia, and under a deep sense of burden from God I was preaching, coming back to my room and kneeling to talk with the Lord. "Show me what You are saying to me about my life."

I was certainly disturbed, and one night I prayed, "Lord, I don't know what's going on." I pulled out a yellow legal pad and drew a circle in the middle with five lines on that paper. And I said, "Lord, You must be saying one of several things." I put the possibilities on each one of those lines and a question mark on the fifth. And I prayed, "Lord, it may be something I have never even thought about."

The next night I knelt down to pray, seeking the will of the Lord. There was a "divine disturbance" going on inside of me. In the midst of my praying it was as though God said, "I am going to move you." When I asked "when?" it seemed to flash across my mind—September. I thought to myself, *Well, this is only April or May. (I had been in Bartow only about eleven months.) Lord, you must be talking about next year. This is a long way ahead of time to inform me."*

And again the following night I started to pray, and there was no burden, nothing to pray about. It was tough. I simply could not become excited.

At the end of the meeting I returned home and shared it with my wife, Anna. The following morning a member of First Church (he's still a member) called me and began the conversation with, "I want to talk with you about something you probably never thought about." And then he mentioned the possibility of my coming to Atlanta, and I answered, "You're right. I never thought about it. Not interested. Don't even want to talk about it, really." I probably accused him of having me on a long list with me close to the bottom, but he replied, "No, I asked the Lord to show me, and you are the only person God has laid on my heart."

"Well, I wouldn't be interested." "Will you pray about

it?" he inquired. I almost nonchalantly answered, "Well, you know I'll pray about it."

I hung up the phone and burst out crying. I thought, *This is ridiculous. I mean, this is absolutely silly.* So, Anna came out to the study and we prayed a while. That was the end of the matter, I was sure.

To make a long story short, on September 30 we moved to Atlanta! Now, I originally did not want to go, but I was highly motivated to be obedient to God. Why? Because I had a clear, unmistakable direction about what God wanted me to do.

You cannot live a rushed, hurried, hectic life, moving all the time, and expect to receive much direction from the Lord. When God saw that Moses was "turned aside," then He spoke to Him. I do not necessarily indicate you will always like His direction, but He will give it to you. One of the most highly motivating factors in obeying is a sense of direction that you know God has spoken clearly.

Daniel realized that God had spoken clearly about what he was to do, and so he was willing to risk his life by humbly challenging the command of the king through his servant, Ashpenaz.

There is a third motivating factor here: *the discovery of what God will do in your life.*

How was Daniel to live in a pagan society with a totally different language, different culture, different lifestyle, where people worshipped pagan gods? How was Daniel to serve a king who would almost identify himself as a god? A king who had the power of life and death over his subjects, who could have them killed at a moment's notice?

What God did was plant in Daniel and his companions a hungering, thirsting, yearning desire to know *how God could use them at that point in their lives.* How could God use one Hebrew teenager to bear a witness for Him in an absolutely totally pagan society which believed that its god was greater than the God of the Hebrews because they had conquered those Hebrews?

Daniel could have alibied, "Well, I guess it's all over." I am sure that crossed Shadrach, Meshach, and Abednego's minds as they faced the fiery furnace. But those young men wisely participated in the education and preparation for service in the king's retinue. For three years they would study in the system in order to discover what Jehovah, Yahweh, Elohim, El-shaddai, the God of glory could do with them in that society.

Have you asked yourself lately, if ever, "What can I do?" Have you talked with the Lord? "God, what could you do with me at this point in this society, if I yielded myself totally to You and withheld nothing from You. What if I gave myself to You without reservation? What could you do with me?"

Does that excite you? Does that motivate you? Or have you already decided to put a clamp and a lid on what God wants to do?

But you may rationalize, "Well, God can't do much with me." Says who? "Well, look at my education."

"Look at my shortage of the social graces." "See how bashful and shy I am." God is not worried about that. God is interested in men and women who are willing to commit themselves to Him without reservation and who have this same sense of commitment Daniel had.

God wants people who will declare, "Lord God, I am committed to obeying You, regardless of the circumstances."

The real question is not what can He do? It is: what will He do if you make a commitment to obey Him at this point in your life, and from this point further by the power of God the Holy Spirit and through the indwelling Christ who is your life? What will God do in and through your life if you follow through on your commitment to Him?

The first time I was ever confronted with that in a forceful manner the Lord had challenged me to do something I did not want to do. You may have picked up the idea that there are many things I don't want to do, which makes it sound like God and I have difficulty getting along. And sometimes we do because of my stubborness. But I am not by myself, am I?

Many times God will challengeus to do something. The prevalent question is not whether or not I want to do it. The ultimate question is: did I or didn't I?

How well I remember when He challenged me with a severely difficult task. I was afraid to confront the situation with a candid approach. I was downright scared, and I prayed, "Lord, I'll get fired if I do that. This'll be the end of my ministry here."

Thus, I had to make a decision, and the time was drawing nigh. I had only a certain amount of days in which to accomplish His task. One morning I was home by myself—Anna was out and the children were at school. I was stretched out on the floor praying and asking for direction. It occurred to me that sometimes we ask for direction, and we do not need to, because God has already given us direction and made that direction plain. When we pray for direction, sometimes we are simply asking, "God, give me the courage to be obedient."

The Lord had been listening to that for at least six months—the same prayer, the same request. That morning, as clearly as a bell, He laid it on the line: "You have two alternatives. You can obey me and allow Me to bless you, or you can choose to disobey Me, and spend the rest of your life wondering what I would have done with you had obeyed Me!"

He motivated me. At the time I was less than thirty years of age, and I said, "Lord, I can't spend the rest of my life wondering what you would have done had I obeyed You at this critical time." When God confronts you, and you have an alternative, He will push you to the brink where you have to make a decision. And it usually boils down to one of two—*to obey or to disobey.*

Never push aside what appears to be a rather unimportant decision. It could be the turning point in your life. There are times when God offers us a choice that will determine how He uses us for the rest of our days. But you have to make the decision.

Have you ever decided that whatever God wants you to do, you are going to do it? Now here is the prayer I began to pray after that day of decision and affirmation of direction. "Lord, I want what You want. When I don't want what You want, You change my wanter, so what You want will become what I want. I want to become locked into Your will. And I may be rebellious at times, and I may not want to do what you say do, but, O God, You put the pressure on me to the extent that ultimately I will have to be obedient, because deep in my heart I really do want to obey You."

With that you can seal yourself in. When you ask the Lord to put the pressure on about obeying Him, rest assured He is not going to forget that plea.

We can become highly motivated by wondering what God would do if we truly obeyed Him. It would be terrible to spend the rest of my life wondering what God would have done if . . . and thus and so. Praise His name, I obeyed Him. To obey God is always the wisest decision.

Yours truly could spend the rest of this book giving you instances of people who have come to me about God's challenges to them in business and every area of life. What God asked them to do seemed insurmountable, impossible, unattainable, and dreadfully risky. They were standing at the crossroads, scared to death about what to do. *When you are obeying God is the only time you are actually secure.*

When you make a leap of faith, you are always going down in the palm of the sovereign hand of God. In Him you are more secure with your eyes closed and going down the side of a mountain than when you are standing on a solid plateau with your eyes wide open. You will never lose by placing your trust in God.

Another highly motivating factor is *our witness before others.* Let us examine this from Daniel 6. Much had transpired since chapter 1. Nebuchadnezzar lost his mind and was succeeded by his son, Belshazzar, who was overthrown and killed by the Medes and Persians. Darius now ruled Babylon and Medo-Persia.

According to verses 1 through 3 Darius had appointed 120 satraps (called princes in the King James) who were to help govern the land. Over those he appointed three presidents, and Daniel was one of the three! Darius preferred Daniel above all of the presidents and princes, and was about to make him his prime minister or number-one man over all of the realm. Suppose Daniel had lost his cool back in chapter 1?

Of course, the princes and presidents were green with jealousy. They sought grounds to accuse Daniel of wrongdoing. They found out that three times a day he opened his window and prayed toward Jerusalem. They sort of remind you of the scribes and Pharisees as they looked for charges against Jesus. Like Pilate with Jesus, they could find no fault with Daniel, so

> these presidents and princes assembled together to the king, and said thus unto him, King Darius, live for ever. All the princes of the kingdom, the governors, and the

princes, the counsellors, and the captains, have consulted together to establish a royal statute, and to make
a firm decree, that whosoever shall ask a petition of any
God or man for thirty days, save of thee, O king, he shall
be cast into the den of lions. Now, O king, establish the
decree, and sign the writing, that it be not changed,
according to the law of the Medes and Persians, which
altereth not. Wherefore king Darius signed the writing
and the decree. (Dan. 6:6-9).

According to the law of the Medes and the Persians,
there was no exception to the law for thirty days, and
even the king could not revoke the statute. Verse 10
states that Daniel knew the writing was signed, so

he went into his house; and his windows being open in
his chamber toward Jerusalem, he kneeled upon his
knees three times a day, and prayed, and gave thanks
before his God, as he did aforetime.

Even faced with the threat of death by vicious beasts,
Daniel continued his prayer life. Why should he
change? Prayer and meditation were second nature to
him. He would continue to commune with the Lord.
Then men representing Daniel's enemies caught Daniel
as he made supplication before his God. Daniel was
arraigned before the king and sentenced to the lions'
den. But even Darius, a heathen king, was confident
about the situation:

Now the king commanded, and they brought Daniel,
and cast him into the den of lions. Now the king spake
unto Daniel, Thy God whom thou servest continually,

he will deliver thee (v. 16).

Can you imagine the witness Daniel already had established with the very king of the empire? "Daniel, I have seen your life, and I know, that even if I throw you into the den of lions, your God is going to come through." Amazing!

Most every Sunday School child knows the story. All night long the king agonized over what he had done to Daniel. His was a night of austerity. He could hardly wait until morning to look in on Daniel.

> Then the king arose very early in the morning, and went in haste unto the den of lions. And when he came to the den, he cried with a lamentable voice unto Daniel: and the king spake and said to Daniel, O Daniel, servant of the living God, is thy God, whom thou servest continually, able to deliver thee from the lions? Then said Daniel unto the king, O king, live for ever. My God hath sent his angel, and hath shut the lions' mouths, that they have not hurt me: forasmuch as before him innocency was found in me; and also before thee, O king, have I done no hurt (vv. 19-22).

When Daniel was thrown into the den of lions, all of the lions had lockjaw. All they could do was smell Daniel, wave their tails, walk around him, perhaps play with him as though they were kitty cats. The tables were turned. After Daniel was retrieved from the den, Darius had Daniel's accusers and their families thrown into the lions' den. Suddenly the lions were healed of their "lockjaw." To make a long story short, the lions devoured Daniel's accusers.

Talk about a success story. Daniel is living proof that it pays to serve the Lord God. Daniel was a winsome witness for the Lord Jesus Christ. The young man knew Him as Jehovah or Elohim and no doubt used different divine names for Him. Daniel bore an unvarnished witness for God in a pagan society.

His commitment to God had motivated him to obediently worship the Lord, recognizing that the exercise of his faith could mean death.

Daniel was brave and courageous. We used to sing that song, "Dare to Be a Daniel, dare to stand alone." Daniel was unafraid of the consequences. Oh, he might have thought about the lions and what it would feel like to be torn into pieces and from limb to limb, but that idea faded in the light of his obedient faith to the God who created those lions.

So many professing Christians live expediently. If they told the truth, they would have to admit, "Yes, I follow the crowd. Which way is the wind blowing? Which way are the people going? Which way is the pressure falling? What will bring me the most approval from my peers? What will keep me from being rejected? What will give me the least amount of harm? The least amount of criticism? And the least amount of the wrong kind of exposure? What is the line of least resistance?"

Committed Christians don't ask those kinds of questions. The committed ask, "Lord, what do you want me to do, regardless of the circumstances or the cost? I leave the consequences up to you, Lord. Period."

You and I are living in a society which reminds us of Babylon in many respects. Even reading the newspaper can make you ill. Our society is filled with ungodliness, vileness, evil, wickedness, demonic and satanic influences.

Have you put special clauses in your commitment to Jesus Christ? A convenience clause? A safety clause? A non-persecution clause? Or have you signed yourself over to Him without a reserve clause. You are committed to Him, even if you are threatened by lions, real or imagined.

To the best of my knowledge, I have never met a true believer who was a "fanatic." What happens is: when we are saved and make a commitment to Jesus Christ to live for Him—and the further and further the world goes away from the standards and truth of the Lord—that makes us look like fanatics when we have not even budged. That is how the world looks at us. Mention the name of Jesus in some circles, and they think you are crazy.

Several years ago you and I could believe what we believe, do what we do as Christians, and guess what? Practically no one would make a case out of it. Today we look like "pious" fanatics. Who has done the moving? Satan and his crowd have done the moving—further and further away from God. The further away they go, the more fanatical we are going to look.

But if you made a commitment never to budge and

never to compromise your convictions for Christ—because of your fear of criticism and approval of your friends—have you joined the world? You comment, "Well, I'm not too far away from where I used to be."

Let me ask you, "Where did your friends go? Are they moving with the unbelieving world?" You must take a stand for Jesus Christ, even if it means losing a few "friends." Your genuine friends will want the best for you and will rejoice that you are living for Christ.

You cannot live according to what certain friends and acquaintances do, but based on what God says. Let me remind you—the further away they move from Christian standards, the worse you look to them, and the holier you look to God.

Another magnificent motivation is *the cause of Christ itself.* Now I want to backtrack to Daniel 5. Belshazzar threw a debauched feast for "a thousand of his lords, and drank wine before the thousand." Belshazzar was like his father, Nebuchadnezzar—perverse. They drank wine from the sacred vessels stolen from the Temple. Little did Belshazzar realize that his moments were numbered. As Belshazzar carried on with his princes, wives, and concubines, Darius was sneaking up on the city.

Amid all of this revelry, fingers of a man's hand began to write on the wall. To this day we use the expression, "the handwriting on the wall," meaning "curtains," "the moment of truth," "doomsday," the "end," and the like. Listen to verse 5:

In the same hour came forth fingers of a man's hand, and wrote over the plaster of the wall of the king's palace: and the king saw the part of the hand that wrote.

Verse 6 records that the king's face grew pale. "His thoughts troubled him, so that the joints of his loins were loosed, and his knees smote one against another." He was "all shook up."

He called all of the astrologers and soothsayers, and none of them could read the writing on the wall. Astrology and fortune telling and the occult are expressly forbidden in the Word of God. They did no good for Belshazzar; neither can they help people today. They are poor substitutes for the truth and wisdom of God as discovered through His Word and the leading of the Holy Spirit.

What happened on that night has figured prominently in the history of civilization. God allowed certain nations to have ascendance—the Egyptians, the Assyrians, the Babylonians, the Medo-Persians, the Greeks, and the Romans. Right here in Daniel is a trail of civilization, God's prophetic work in all of human history. What transpired on that fateful night was a part of what God was doing in the world. Then Daniel came on the scene in verse 16, upon recommendation of the queen, who had called him "a man in thy kingdom, in whom is the spirit of the holy gods." Daniel was temporarily on the shelf, but now he was called forth again.

And I have heard of thee, that thou canst make interpretations and dissolve doubts: now if thou canst read the writing, and make known to me the interpretation thereof, thou shalt be clothed with scarlet, and have a chain of gold about thy neck, and shalt be the third ruler in the kingdom.

Belshazzar made all kinds of promises, and was not even aware that he would be unable to fulfill most of them, even if Daniel had wanted them.

Then Daniel answered and said before the king, Let thy gifts be to thyself, and give thy rewards to another; yet I will read the writing unto the king, and make known to him the interpretation. O thou king, the most high God gave Nebuchadnezzar thy father a kingdom, and majesty, and glory, and honour: And for the majesty that he gave him, all people, nations, and languages, trembled and feared before him: whom he would he slew; and whom he would he kept alive; and whom he would he set up; and whom he would he put down. (5:16-19)

Daniel continued to speak about Nebuchadnezzar lifting up his pride and becoming hardened, and the fact that Nebuchadnezzar became deranged and roamed through the fields like an animal and eating grass. "He was deposed from his kingly throne, and they took his glory away from him" (v. 20). Only when Nebuchadnezzar acknowledged that the most high God ruled in the kingdom of mankind was he restored to his mental health (see v. 21).

And thou his son, O Belshazzar, hast not humbled thine heart, though thou knewest all this; But hast lifted up thyself against the Lord of heaven; and they have brought the vessels of his house before thee, and thou, and thy lords, thy wives, and thy concubines, have drunk wine in them; and thou hast praised the gods of silver, and gold, of brass, iron, wood, and stone, which see not, nor hear, nor know: and the God in whose hand are all thy ways, hast thou not glorified (vv. 22-23).

Then Daniel interpreted the handwriting: MENE, MENE, TEKEL, UPHARSIN. MENE meant that God had numbered Belshazzar's kingdom and finished it (v. 26). TEKEL meant that he was "weighed in the balances, and art found wanting" (v. 27). PERES (which was a form of UPHARSIN) meant that "thy kingdom is divided, and given to the Medes and Persians" (v. 28). And Belshazzar insisted on following through on his promises to Daniel,

Informing Belshazzar concerning the true meaning of the handwriting was not pleasant. Who wants to inform a person of impending calamity? Who wants to carry the news of death to a home? Who wants to be the harbinger of bad tidings? Daniel could have played ignorant, but there was a compulsion to be God's messenger.

Are you willing to obey God regardless of the consequences, even if it means your neck, even if it leads to ridicule or rejection? That is why so many preachers preach sweetness and light. It is not pleasant to preach condemnation and judgment, hell and punishment, but it is mandatory if we are following the will of God. Are you willing to confront people with the truth of Jesus

Christ, whether or not they like you? Do you hesitate to bear witness for Jesus Christ because you are afraid folks will reject you?

Like Daniel, you have the only message which can transform the world. What keeps you from sharing this message boldly, lovingly, pointedly, effectively, courageously, fruitfully with people who need to be saved?

As a teenager Daniel purposed in his heart to be obedient to Jehovah God. Have you done that?

Now have you ever honestly made a commitment, saying to Him, "Lord, I will obey you, come what may"? Or are you playing around with the providence of God?

After all is said and done, a sincere, committed child of God will ultimately ask one primary question: What will it take for me to be obedient to God? Then, as God shows you, answer *yes*. When we love the Christ and His cause, we will make an irrevocable stand.

You remember I had a covenant with God—still do: "God, put the pressure on me to keep me in the pathway and following You without reservation and hesitation." If God has not put any pressure on you, you have an exhilarating experience in store. If you are His child, He will have to exercise His constraint on you. God should not have to motivate you by pressure, but He will if He has to. The more compulsion you feel, the more pressure, the more important it is in the economy of God. We hear about "laid-back" Christians. I never knew a totally committed Christian who was laid back. There is a compulsion, a compunction, a constraint.

There is an urgency about doing God's will.

What will it finally take to motivate you into making this commitment to Jesus Christ?

Right now will you, in your own words and in your own way, make a commitment to Him? "Lord Jesus, I commit myself to You, that by the power of the Holy Spirit and the indwelling Christ, I will obey You regardless of the consequences."

No one, not even God, can force you into that commitment. But you should make it because of who you are and Who He is—and because of His purpose in your life.

Will you do that now?

CHAPTER 4

Resistance to Commitment

Jonah

If we believe God is Who He declares He is, and if He wants only the best for us, why would we ever resist being committed to Him? We ask that question, "Why?" and even while we ask it, we can point out times in our lives when we definitely knew the plan and purpose of God for us—and yet deliberately, willfully resisted God. Why would we do that?

Jonah is the epitome of a person who knew exactly what God was calling him to do, and yet resisted and rebelled against that call. If you are a modern-day Jonah, God will convict you by continuing to surface the issue of your call and commitment. Every time you try to pray, God reminds you of your calling from Him. What finally happens is that we deal with the matter, or we cease to pray. That has transpired in the lives of many backslidden Christians.

Through Jonah we will learn why we sometimes resist our commitment to God.

Now the word of the Lord came unto Jonah the son of

Amittai, saying, Arise, go to Nineveh, that great city, and cry against it; for their wickedness is come up before me (1:1-2).

Nineveh had a population of around six hundred thousand people, one hundred twenty thousand of them probably children, according to the fourth chapter of Jonah. God gave inescapable, unmistakable instructions to Jonah—"Go and cry against Nineveh."

But what did he do in the light of God's clear commission?

But Jonah rose up to flee unto Tarshish [Spain]: so he paid the fare thereof, and went down into it, to go with them unto Tarshish from the presence of the Lord (v. 3).

Anytime you are running from the presence of the Lord, you are going down. He went *down* to Joppa, *down* to inside the ship. Down, down, down. So, the Scripture then records in verse 4:

But the Lord sent out a great wind into the sea, and there was a mighty tempest in the sea, so that the ship was like to be broken.

Verse 5 presents the terror of the seamen, who began to lighten the ship by throwing the baggage and wares overboard. "But Jonah was gone down [down again] into the sides of the ship; and he lay, and he was fast asleep.

Then, in verse 6 the shipmaster, the captain of the ship, called out, "What do you mean?" He called Jonah "sleeper." He continued, "Arise, call upon thy God, if so be that God will think upon us, that we perish not." The captain and crew seemed to understand more about Jehovah God than Jonah did at that moment.

In their false religion and supersitition, however, they wanted to cast lots or draw straws to discover who was responsible for the calamity which had befallen them. They cast lots, and the lot fell on none other than Jonah, disobedient, rebellious Jonah.

They zeroed in on the prophet in verses 8 through 15. In verse 9 Jonah confessed that he was a Hebrew, that he feared the Lord who had created the sea and the land.

> Then were the men exceedingly afraid, and said unto him, Why hast thou done this? For the men knew that he fled from the presence of the Lord, because he had told them (v. 10).

So filled with guilt was he that he suggested they throw him overboard, realizing that the sea would become calm, "for I know that for my sake this great tempest is upon you" (see vv. 11-12). The men were humane enough not to accept his suggestion at first. They rowed hard and tried to reach land, but to no avail (see v. 13).

Then they began to cry unto the Lord, not their own powerless gods, "We beseech thee, O Lord, we beseech thee, let us not perish for this man's life, and lay not upon us innocent blood: for thou, O Lord, hast done as it pleased thee" (v. 14). Finally (v. 15) they felt there was no recourse, so they cast Jonah overboard. "The sea ceased her raging" when they threw him into the ocean. The reason many of you are raging with a tempest on the inside is: There is a Jonah within—that in your life which you will not commit and surrender, which you will not give up, which you will not face. You absolutely refuse to confront it and deal with it, and the storm keeps on raging. Yet, you insist on petting that which is foreign to the will of God.

We have reason to believe that Jehovah had converts among those seamen. They had seen the hand of the Almighty as the storm had subsided. They had a service of praise and thanksgiving to express gratitude to the God of the universe, YHWH. They offered a sacrifice and made vows (see v. 16).

In the King James Version there recurs the phrase, "And the Lord prepared . . ." At first He prepared a great fish, called a whale in the New Testament.

> Now the Lord had prepared a great fish to swallow Jonah. And Jonah was in the belly of the fish three days and three nights (v. 17).

Jonah was in profound distress. People have debated and disputed the account about a fish or whale's swallowing Jonah. That fish did. Since God prepared it, perhaps there has not been another fish quite like it in the history of the world. Regardless, the fish swallowed Jonah. Make no mistake about it. People have commented, "Good grief, no one could live in the belly of a fish or whale for three days and three nights." Jonah did. Anyhow, there have been accounts of people being swallowed who have lived.

You mark how quickly Jonah became prayerful and righteous. He prayed unto the Lord his God out of the belly of that fish. "And said, I cried by reason of mine affliction unto the Lord, and he heard me; out of the belly of hell cried I, and thou heardest my voice" (2:2).

There Jonah was covered by the waters which were drunk by the fish. All kinds of sea creatures probably sloshed around in there with him—small fish, squid, mollusks, and the like. The seaweed was wrapped around his head. In verses 4-6 his agonies are enumerated. A nauseous dread, a terrifying panic, had set in.

> Then I said, I am cast out of thy sight; yet I will look again toward thy holy temple. The waters compassed me about, even to the soul: the depths closed me round about, the weeds were wrapped around my head. I went down to the bottoms of the mountains; the earth with her bars was about me for ever: yet hast thou brought up my life from corruption, O Lord, my God.

It was as though Jonah were in a horrid pit. It was a living death.

Can you remember those times when going was smooth, and then you began to take God's blessings for granted? You presumed on His goodness, and you bypassed His clear-cut commandment and commission for you. Then you were swallowed up, not by a whale, but by adversity and calamity. With your back against the wall, where else could you turn, and what else could you do? You threw yourself before God and yelled for His help. And you remember how you had disappointed and embarrassed Him, how you had rebelled against His crystal-clear assignments for you.

> When my soul fainted within me I remembered the Lord; and my prayer came in unto thee, into thine holy temple. They that observe lying vanities forsake their own mercy. But I will sacrifice unto thee with the voice of thanksgiving; I will pay that that I have vowed. Salvation is of the Lord (vv. 7-9).

In verse 9 he was actually promising that he would go to Nineveh. Out of his desperation, he was vowing: "Lord, I will go to that heathen city. The fact is, I'll go anywhere. I'll do anything. Just give me the word." Does that sound familiar? Have you done that? You have given the Lord a hard time, and you have sidestepped His call and commission, literally rebelling against Him. And He has had to send the whale which covered you up, smothering you, and you have felt that death was upon you. As Jonah did: even in the dark, you saw the light.

Jonah took that ride in the whale because of his rebellion. As a prophet he had once committed himself to the Lord, but God had made a further call, and Jonah had run from it.

We have done exactly the same. The problems and pressures weight down on us, and we holler to the Lord, "Lord, I don't know why I'm in this mess." If we were disobedient to His call, we know why. There is no point playing ignorant with the Lord.

While we are healthy, strong, and in control, it is easy to put the Lord off: "Not now, Lord, and not this. No way. I'm not going where you want me to go. I'm not going to witness in the seedy side of town. I'm not going to accept that assignment at a mission. I'm not going to that little church. I'm not going to that challenging church. If I do I won't have enough time for golf and hunting and fishing and having a good time."

Ah, but when we are in the belly of the whale, and it looks as though we are goners, that's different. You finally become obedient. I beg of you not to force God's hand and practically make Him send the whale.

It is remarkable that at the very moment Jonah cried, "Salvation is of the Lord," the Lord "spake unto the fish, and it vomited out Jonah upon the dry land" (vv. 9-10). That was special delivery; Jonah did not even have to swim to shore. The whale vomited him onto *dry land.* Now let us look at Jonah's recommission:

> And the word of the Lord came unto Jonah the second time, saying, Arise go unto Nineveh, that great city, and preach unto it the preaching that I bid thee (3:1-2).

God did not have to come back the third time—only the second.

> So Jonah arose, and went unto Nineveh, according to the word of the Lord, Now Nineveh was an exceeding great city of three days' journey (v. 3).

Talk about area. The city was so vast that it would require three days for Jonah to walk through it! So Jonah began his walking preaching tour:

> And Jonah began to enter into the city a day's journey, and he cried, and said, Yet forty days, and Nineveh shall be overthrown (v. 4).

Jonah finally obeyed God. Why would Jonah resist his commitment to the Lord? An even better question is: Why would you?

One of the primary reasons we resist and refuse to fulfill our commitment to God is: *we are afraid.*

We become fearful, first of all, *because we might fail.* We are fearful of failure, afraid of criticism. *What will they think if I don't measure up to people's expectations?* And we are frightened of exposure—that folks are going to spot our faults, that we are not as good as we ought to be, that we are not capable and efficient as we should be.

The act of faith is being willing to place your trust in the wisdom and the will of God without knowing the outcome. If you were already able to predict the outcome, you would rule out the role of faith.

Chapter 3, beginning with verse 5, relates the repentance of the Ninevites. "They proclaimed a fast, and put on sackcloth, from the greatest of them even to the least of them" (v. 5). The king led out by covering himself with sackcloth and sprinkling ashes on his head, and he declared a national day (or period) of fasting and repentance:

And he proclaimed and published through Nineveh by the decree of the king and his nobles, saying, Let neither man nor beast, herd nor flock, taste any thing: let them not feed, nor drink water: But let man and beast be covered with sackcloth, and cry mightily unto God: yea, let them turn every one from his evil way, and from the violence that is in their hands. Who can tell if God will turn and repent, and turn away from his fierce anger, that we perish not? And God saw their works, that they turned from their evil way; and God repented of the evil, that he had said unto them that he would do unto them; and he did it not (vv. 7-10).

One aspect of Jonah's initial refusal to go was exactly this: he was afraid that if he preached repentance and salvation to the wicked people of Nineveh, they would repent and turn to God. Deep down inside he must have resented the thought of it—that those filthy heathens could be recipients of the grace he had already abundantly received!

On the surface you would think that Jonah would have been celebrating the Ninevites' repentance, leaping and praising God with "Hallelujah!" and "Glory to God!" Oh, no. Could you imagine a sane preacher of the gospel not being thrilled when thousands accepted his invitation to repent and to be delivered from divine wrath? But not Jonah. He did not even thank God for using him as an instrument of God's grace.

His response to their repentance is incredible:

But it displeased Jonah exceedingly, and he was very angry (4:1).

Can you believe that kind of attitude? He was incensed and also pouting that those people were saved! In essence, he argued with the Lord, "Look, Lord, didn't I tell You, even before I left my own country, what was going to happen—that these people were going to repent when I preached to them? But You insisted that I go ahead."

> I pray thee, O Lord, was not this my saying, when I was yet in my country? Therefore I fled before unto Tarshish: for I knew that thou art a gracious God, and merciful, slow to anger, and of great kindness, and repentest thou of the evil (v. 2).

Jonah's problem was not fear of failure. It was fear of success! "Lord, if I preach Your message, it will succeed. The people will repent and be saved. They will get right with You." Jonah was a weird fellow. Jonah's root problem was: he was afraid that God would do something Jonah did not want Him to do.

Most of us resist commitment because we are afraid to fail, afraid of criticism, exposure, the unknown. We are afraid of what is going to happen, and we have no idea what is going to transpire. Jonah knew what was going to happen when he preached the message.

Many times God may have called you to certain tasks for Him, and often you have paraded before Him all the dire possibilities. After you have tried to build up your case, then you pray, "Lord, there is no way for me to do that. Suppose any of these things happen to me? Then, what will be the result?"

Often we want a detailed road map before following His assignment. "Now, God, just tell me what's going to happen, and assure me that everything is going to be all right, and then I'll do it." It just doesn't work like that. That is not obedience; that is not faith; that is trying to fit God into your matrix and mold, endeavoring to make the Omnipotent God of glory fit into your little two-by-four schemes! When you operate from that stance, it is definitely by sight and not faith.

How many blessings have you missed because you were afraid to trust God? What have you overlooked in your business because of your lack of faith, in your relationships to others? Because you would not open up and be transparently honest, you have lost out on deep, abiding fellowship and friendship. What have you missed because you would not turn loose of your money and release it to God?

If you wait to "get my ducks in a row," you will never serve the Lord with a profound commitment. Unless you let God have charge and quit finagling with His will, you will devastatingly fail in His eyes!

There is a second reason why we fail to follow through on our commitments, and that is old-fashioned selfishness, the kind that originated with Lucifer, the kind that precipitated the fall in the Garden of Eden. "Is this what You want me to do, Lord? Really, now, that doesn't fit into *my* plans." Most of the time we might not verbalize that inwardly or outwardly, but that is what we mean. We nonchalantly and quietly go about our own business as though God never existed, as though God were dead. What we are indicating is: "Lord, Your plan doesn't fit *my* plan. I choose *my* plan over Your plan." That is disastrous.

I have already alluded to Jonah's prejudice. He had a bitter distaste for the Ninevites. They posed a serious military threat to the Israelites. God's call to Jonah was similar to a modern preacher of the gospel being summoned to preach the gospel to the Communists in Russia, Red China, Cambodia, Bulgaria, or even Afghanistan.

And Jonah's response was similar to a modern preacher who would pontificate: "Why preach to them? Look what the rascals have done, look at the people they have persecuted and exterminated. Why, we don't want a revival over there. We want God to wipe them out!" Do you remember when the disciples asked Jesus to call down fire and brimstone on the Samaritans?

Jonah did not want them to repent. Rather he wanted them destroyed and wiped from the face of the earth. We have analyzed 4:1-2 where Jonah expressed his anger and spoke about his detour toward Tarshish, reminding the Lord that He is gracious, merciful, slow to anger, and kind. Guess what? Jonah was so upset he prayed to die. He worked himelf into a suicidal death wish. Why? Because he was not pleased with the outcome. The people repented, and he despised the thought of it.

Quite frankly, God had every reason to take his life. It

is hard to envision a more rebellious, stubborn man of God in the entire Bible. He moaned: "Therefore now, O Lord, take, I beseech thee, my life from me; for it is better for me to die than to live" (v. 3).

> So Jonah went out of the city, and sat on the east side of the city, and there made him a booth [a lean-to], and sat under it in the shadow, till he might see what would become of the city (v. 5).

Can you believe it? He had not given up. He was still hoping that God would annihilate the Ninevites. He sat out there like a vulture and smacked his parched lips, planning to sit out there for forty days. Within forty days, God was going to destroy the city *if* its inhabitants did not repent, but massive repentance was going on back in Nineveh.

When God prepares something it is well-prepared. He had prepared that great fish or whale. Now He prepared . . .

> . . . a gourd, and made it to come up over Jonah, that it might be a shadow over his head, to deliver him from his grief. So Jonah was exceeding glad of the gourd (v. 6).

A gourd vine was provided to protect the rebellious, pouting prophet from the hot Middle-Eastern sun. But God was not finished with His preparation.

> But God prepared a worm when the morning rose the next day, and it smote the gourd that it withered (v. 7).

What twisted priorities! Jonah was ecstatic over the

plant which gave him momentary comfort from the heat. It reminds you of modern Christians obsessed with air conditioning while their friends and neighbors are going to the furnace of hell. Jonah, bless his heart, was "exceedingly glad of the gourd." So God prepared or appointed something else special—a little worm. That worm taught a spiritual object lesson. God can use the biggest or littlest creatures for His glory. The worm nibbled on that big, tree-like plant, and it withered.

There Jonah was, waiting for the fire of destruction to fall on Nineveh (and it did not until many years later), and caring more for that gourd plant than eternal souls.

Aha, God prepared something more—a sirocco, that burning, scorching east wind which sweeps across the desert of the Middle East like the flames of a blast furnace.

> And it came to pass, when the sun did arise, that God prepared a vehement east wind; and the sun beat upon the head of Jonah, that he fainted, and wished in himself to die, and said, it is better for me to die than to live (v. 8).

There was his death wish again—and all because he was not getting his way.

God then asked Jonah, "Do you have a good reason to be all angry and pouty about this plant?" And Jonah replied, "I surely do. Why, I'm so mad I want to die!" (see v. 9). Then the Lord, in love and not lambasting, answered, "Thou hast had pity on the gourd, for the which thou hast not labored, neither madest it grow;

which came up in the night, and perished in a night" (v. 10).

And the Book of Jonah ends almost abruptly with the final rebuke from the Lord.

> And should not I spare Nineveh, that great city, wherein are more than six-score thousand persons that cannot discern between their right hand and their left hand; and also much cattle? (v. 11).

From all of the foregoing, what can we learn? We can realize there are times we resist commitment to the Lord because we have our own plans and sytems worked out, and we do not want God controlling our lives. We are often downright selfish over our little gourd vines, our pets, our cozy pleasures and follies. And we are often prejudiced, not merely toward the person of another race, but prejudiced toward anyone who is different from us—seemingly not as "spiritual," not at cultured, not as educated, not as refined, "from the other side of the tracks."

We oftentimes disobey God because we have His plans misfigured. We are afraid what will happen if we follow through on our commitment.

If God commands you to do something, He knows the beginning, the middle, the end, the ultimate results. And if He is instructing you to do something, it is for a divine reason—which you and I are not to question, but to obey.

There is no doubt that Jonah made all kinds of alibis to the Lord, even though they are not detailed here. It was a long trip to Nineveh. it was inconvenient, costly, dangerous, uncomfortable. It did not fit into his plans. Robbers could swoop down on people en route. One could fall and hurt himself. The predominant reason was, and Jonah did not try to deny it, *selfishness.* It reminds us of the song, "I Did It My Way."

What is keeping you from being obedient to the Holy God? Maybe He has called on you to do something about your marriage. Husband, you used that old out, "She doesn't understand me. She doesn't try to please me," and you may have tried to justify your leaving home. Wife, maybe he has been unfaithful to you, but now he has repented. He wants to come back, but you continue to vent your displeasure without trying to forgive him: "After what he's done to me and the kids, I can't take him back." Perhaps you are one who ought to straighten out a marriage.

Our selfishness, like Jonah's, will veritably consume us.

We must ask, "Lord, what did I commit myself to?" The answer: "I committed myself to living in submission to Your divine authority, Lord, whether I liked it or not." And as you develop and grow, you will learn to like it.

There is a third reason we resist commitment to God: *we have a poor self-image.* We moan and groan, "Oh, God, not me. You've got to be kidding. You're talking about somebody else. Somebody else, Lord. I'm no good."

That was not Jonah's reply, but that is often ours. I

realize that many use that cop-out as an excuse. Throughout the Bible the called servants of God came up with excuses—Moses, Jeremiah, Ananias who baptized Paul, Peter, ad infinitum.

Gideon also suffered from a poor self-image and lack of confidence. In Judges 6, when the angel of the Lord "appeared unto him, and said unto him, The Lord is with thee, thou mighty man of valour," he excused himself with, "O my Lord, if the Lord be with us, why then is all this befallen us?" (vv. 12-13).

Even the mightiest men and women of the Bible expressed lack of confidence, self-doubt. Today we alibi, "Why, Lord, I don't have the ability. I'm so inadequate, shaky, unequipped."

People who are inadequate outside of God's power are those He is seeking—adequate in Him but totally incompetent and inadequate without Him.

When God calls you, He will enter the middle of your life and take your hand, walking with you every single step. All He asks is your commitment and your willingness, through His power, to follow through on that commitment.

Now let us notice *how we resist Him.* We are afraid, we are selfish, we have a poor self-image. But how did we come about these factors? Now, I doubt if you shook your fist at the Lord and screamed, "Lord, I heard what You said, but I'm not going to do it. I'm not going to obey You." Your eyes did not glaze over, and you did not foam at the mouth. Even though some may have done that, I doubt if you, as a Christian, did.

But many believers have shaken their hearts in God's face. Deep down inside they have put on a last-ditch battle: "I'm not gonna do it. I'm not gonna go to my Nineveh. Call somebody else."

How do we go about resisting God? First, *we argue with Him.* We put up more arguments than the most-skilled debaters in Parliament or the House of Representatives. God has heard them all already. Quit trying to be creative and original! He has heard them clear back to Eden. It is heartbreaking, but most of God's leaders in the Bible argued with Him on occasion. You may not argue with Him heatedly, but you may argue nonetheless.

But next of all, we may not actually argue with Him. This is more subtle. We say, "Yes, Lord, sure enough. I heard what You are saying." But what we do is *make a substitute.* We substitute our plan for God's plan, and we refuse to call that resistance. Oh, but it is.

In 1 Samuel there is a prime example of substitution. The Lord commanded Saul "to utterly destroy all that they [the Amalekites] have, and spare them not; but slay both man and woman, infant and suckling, ox and sheep, camel and ass." Remember that the Amalekites were vicious, ungodly people set on totally destroying the Israelites. Now, you recall the story of Saul's partial obedience. "But Saul and the people spared Agag, and the best of the sheep, and of the oxen, and of the fatlings, and the lambs, and all that was good, and would not utterly destroy them: but every thing that was vile and refuse, that they destroyed utterly."

Saul did not argue with the Lord about this strategy. He simply obeyed partially as a substitute, thinking nothing would come of it. When Samuel, the representative of the Lord, found out, he delivered a scathing denunciation concerning Saul's leadership. Samuel then carried out the total destruction of Agag, the king of the Amalekites, and all of the spoil Saul had improperly kept.

Saul did not argue, but he made a disobedient substitute for total obedience.

All around us are people who are working like crazy, and becoming caught up in all kinds of projects and activities, to keep from devoting themselves, their time and energy to the Lord's cause. They figure that if they work hard enough and run fast enough, finally the Lord will leave them alone, and let them do their own "stuff," as the kids put it. God is not going to bless that runaround. He demands commitment and obedience.

Obedience is working out the plan of God in your life and walking a straight line for Him—no circuitous routes, no side trips, no detours. Jonah detoured en route to Spain. Saul devised his own convenient plan. You and I have done the same.

Let me ask, Are you walking in obedience to God this very moment? Or have you rushed in your own spurious substitute? We often sound like Saul, "Hey, here's what we're going to do. There's no sense in wasting these choice animals. Why, we can sacrifice them to God. We wouldn't want to waste them."

I have heard this story repeatedly, to the point it makes me sick at the stomach. "Yes, the Lord called me to preach when I was twenty-one, but *I* decided *I* was going into business, and *I* was gonna make a whole lot of money, so I could give big bucks to missions." Sounds like Saul, does it not? No matter how good Saul's plans, and our substitutes, sound, that is still rebellion and resistance against God.

You will never please God until you follow His instructions to the letter, until you start right at square one where God wants you. And remember that *partial obedience is still disobedience to God.*

Do you realize why so many Christians have so little power? They have become so confused about their plans and God's that they cannot distinguish what God wants, and they have no grasp of what God has commanded them to do. They are that confused and misguided.

It is tragic that this attitude will rub off on your children and your kinfolks—also on your friends. Many a parent has compromised before his children. The father of the home, trying to keep as much money as he can, sums it up: "Well, now, I know we're supposed to give a tithe—ten percent. And I'm willing to do it. But here's what we'll do. We'll give two percent over there, and three percent over there, and four percent over there, and the like. We're going to give it our way and to our own thing.

We'll give the church part of that tithe."

And another father rationalizes the situation: "I believe the tithe should include what you give to the United Way and to social causes, you know. If you see somebody in need, give them part of your tithe." Now God declared, "Bring ye all the tithes into the storehouse," and he calls on us to give tithes and offerings to His cause. That type of excusing oneself will not mesh with the plan of God. It is an act of skillful disobedience to God. God owns all of it and requires that I give a certain portion, without strings attached, to His work.

I have listened to scores of men and women who decided on another plan but the plan of God. Sometimes it was many years ago; others recently. Never have I seen such crestfallen, miserable people. One man confessed, "For ten long years I have been having it my way, and now I am miserable and wretched!" If you are born again, if you have ever committed yourself to the Lord Jesus, and if you compromise and substitute, it will eventually take a terrible toll on you.

In addition to arguing with Him or substituting our plan for His, *we can deny His call altogether.* I hear that all the time, "Well, I was down praying about my life, and God told me to do something, but I backed off from that. I consulted with the guys at the office, and I talked with my wife, and I batted it around. And, you know, God really didn't say that after all."

Do not depend on your friends about the call of God. Depend on your Friend, the Lord Jesus Christ. Let me give you a personal example. I can remember one particular occasion when I was facing one of the most crucial decisions of my life, and I gave my wife this long "spiel," a Saul spiel. I had worked hard on my alibis after praying over the matter for a long while. Boy, my case surely sounded good, and I laid it on my wife. She looked at me and asked, "Did God tell you that?"

Case closed! That was the end of my spiel, because God had not told me that.

Now carefully consider this principle. *If God tells you to do something you fall on your knees and seek His mind about it. What you get while on your knees is far safer than what you get while standing up.* Now, there are exceptions if you have bone disease or arthritis. Even if you cannot bow your body, bow your heart.

Satan is going to give you all kinds of ideas how you can violate God's will when you are away from the place of prayer.

Sometimes we not only deny the commission of God—*we simply run from it.* This is what Jonah did. He found a ship going to Spain because it was the farthest distance he could think of, and it was in the opposite direction from Nineveh. Why did he head toward Spain—because of a guilty conscience? Why did he jump on that ship?—conscience! Why did he fall asleep in the ship? Conscience. Why did he ask them to cast him into the sea? The same. He was running from the Lord, even though he clearly knew God's will—and his conscience was killing him.

Are you haunted by a feeling of guilt? In the morning, at noon, in the night? Do you doubt God's love from time to time, even though you must recognize He does love you? Do you feel that God is not pleased—and He may not be—but He loves you?

This gnawing deep inside your vitals stays with you. Could it be your conscience keeps gnawing away, "Disobedient! Disobedient! Disobedient!" Maybe that eating away continues, but you muffle and stifle it. You beg it to go away, and it becomes fainter and fainter, and dimmer and dimmer. You are in a deadly, dangerous position when you cannot hear it.

What does it cost to deny God's will in your life? First, *it costs you peace.* There is not a Christian on the face of the earth who can have inner peace and live in disobedience and rebellion to God. You cannot be at peace when you are at war with God!

Secondly, *you lose your joy.* You fall out of fellowship with God. That happened to David. He never prayed: "Restore unto me thy salvation," but "restore unto me the *joy* of thy salvation" (Ps. 51:12*a.*). You begin to lose your power in serving the Lord. Perhaps at one time you were winning souls to Christ, and that seldom, if ever, happens now. You begin to lose your opportunity. Maybe even your health and your finances.

Every day you and I live outside the authority of Jesus Christ as Lord of our lives, failing to follow the commitment he asks from us, we are paying awful interest on the debt. Every day you live away from His good and acceptable and perfect will, you are storing up regret and remorse which will bear agony and misery now and later.

The interest is worse than 20 percent or 30 percent. It is 100 percent. What has it already cost you, dear friend, not to fulfill God's will for your life? How often I hear from people with tears streaming down their cheeks, "Oh, if only somebody had told me all of this years ago!" But it is too late now. They can serve the Lord, yes, but not as fully and as lengthily as they could years before when they sidestepped His plans and wishes. They had to make a living, but they failed to make a life. "They all with one accord began to make excuse."

Yes, God will forgive you. But you have already lost opportunities you cannot summon back.

Right now, as much as you are aware in your heart, are you walking in obedience? Is your life fulfilling the will of God? If it is not, I challenge you to go back and find the place where you left the track, climb back on, and confess to God:

"Lord, from this point on, no more running. Just trusting You, believing You. Trusting my future in Your hands. I don't understand the circumstances, but here is my life, dear God. I submit to Your authority, Lord, and I leave the cricumstances and consequences in Your hands."

C H A P T E R 5

Commitment on Trial

Genesis 22:1-12

No matter how committed you are to Jesus Christ, somewhere along the line that commitment is going to be tested.

If ever a man was committed to the Lord God, it was Abraham, the father of the Hebrew nation and a prime exponent of faith. One statement we most often remember about Abraham is in Romans 4:3: "For what saith the scripture? Abraham believed God, and it was counted unto him for righteousness." Think of faith, and your mind is automatically drawn to Abraham.

In spite of his abiding and enduring faith, Abraham was put to one of the most stringent tests ever faced by a believer.

As you will recall, Abraham was called out of a pagan land, Ur of the Chaldees. He was asked to leave his background, his home, his kinfolks, his customs, and his old religion. The Word of God speaks concerning his emigration from Ur:

By faith Abraham, when he was called to go out into a

place which he should after receive for an inheritance, obeyed; and he went out, not knowing whither he went (Heb. 11:8).

Time and again his faith was tested, and he remained steadfast and true. He had his faults—he could lie, and he did that twice concerning his wife Sarai (later Sarah), calling her his sister—but one of them was not lack of faith. He believed God with most, if not 100 percent, of his being. In our text God had carried him to the most crucial, agonizing test of his entire life:

And it came to pass after these things that God did tempt [test] Abraham, and said unto him, Abraham: and he said, Behold, here I am (Gen. 22:1).

Does that sound familiar? The Bible characters who seemed to glorify God the most were ready and willing to answer, "Here I am." Moses, Isaiah, Jacob, Paul, and others. That phrase carries with it more than the idea of location—it denotes love. "I love you. Lord God, so I am available to you." That is commitment right off the bat.

And he said, Take now thy son, thine only son Isaac, whom thou lovest, and get thee into the land of Moriah; and offer him there for a burnt offering upon one of the mountains which I will tell thee of. And Abraham rose up early in the morning, and saddled his ass, and took two of his young men with him, and Isaac his son, and clave the wood for the burnt offering, and rose up, and went unto the place of which God had told him. Then on the third day Abraham lifted up his eyes and saw the place afar off. And Abraham said unto his young men,

Abide ye here with the ass; and I and the lad will go yonder and worship, and come again unto you (vv. 2-5).

In the Hebrew the text states, "We will worship, and we will return." Even though God had commanded him to "offer him [Isaac] there as a burnt sacrifice," Abraham seemed to indicate that the two of them would come back from the altar of worship.

And Abraham took the wood of the burnt offering and laid it upon Isaac his son; and he took the fire in his hand, and a knife; and they went both of them together (v. 6).

You can imagine what Abraham was thinking as he and his only son, Isaac, were going toward the place of sacrifice.

And Isaac spake unto Abraham his father, and said, My father: and he said, Behold Here am I, my son. And he said, Behold the fire and the wood: but where is the lamb for a burnt offering? (v. 7.)

Isaac was submissive to his father, but he wondered about the sacrifice. Do you suppose he thought, *Other peoples around us sacrifice their children. Is that what my father is going to do with me?* Of course, we will never know—not in this life, anyhow.

There must have been a lump in Abraham's throat and a tear in his eye when he replied, "My son, God will provide himself a lamb for a burnt offering" (v. 8). They continued to walk toward the altar, with Isaac carrying the wood that would soon be aflame.

> And they came to the place which God had told him of;
> and Abraham built an altar there, and laid the wood in
> order, and bound Isaac on the altar upon the wood.
> And Abraham stretched forth his hand, and took the
> knife to slay his son. And the angel of the Lord called
> unto him out of heaven, and said, Abraham, Abraham:
> and he said, Here am I (vv. 9-11).

Do you notice Abraham's response? Availability. Submissiveness. Obedience. No complaint. No question. No rationalization. No argumentation. No asking of "why?"

> And he said, Lay not thine hand upon the lad, neither
> do thou any thing unto him: for now I know that thou
> fearest God, seeing thou hast not withheld thy son,
> thine only son from me (v. 12).

All of you are familiar with the rest of the story. Every one of us is going to be tested and tried somewhere along the line.

Are you committed to the Lord Jesus Christ, understanding that His Lordship means that you acknowledge His right to have final authority in all your life's decisions? Is He truly Lord in your life?

Are you completely sold out to Him in body, soul, and spirit? Are you available to Him? Do you mean business?

God tested Abraham in a most unique manner. I doubt if He is going to test You in the same fashion.

There is practically no chance that He will ask you to prepare one of your children for a sacrifice, but *you will be tested.* And what we have to examine in the light of this passage is: "Lord, how do you test me in my commitment to You?"

As I point out more than once in these pages, all of us are at different levels of commitment. Abraham was in the upper echelons of commitment and unswerving obedience. I doubt if a one of us has reached the level of Abraham's commitment and availability to God. But we ought to be moving and growing in that direction.

The first question I want to pose is this: *Why does God test your commitment?*

Why should God, who is omniscient, have to test me in order to find out about my commitment? The reason God tests our commitment is not *to discover how committed we are.* The fact is: He already knows. So why the test?

I trust that you have a certain level of commitment as a believer, and you are committed at different levels at different times in your life.

First, let us consider *purpose.* I feel there are two reasons God will test our commitment to Him, even though He is already well aware of how we are going to respond. The first is: *God wants to reveal certain concepts to us.* Naturally, you are asking, "What in the world does He want to reveal to us?" And what did He want to reveal to Abraham?

One of the pivotal purposes for which God will test

our commitment is *that we might find out how committed we ourselves are.* Not long ago I would have testified, if you had asked, "I am committed, probably more committed than I have ever been in my life and ministry." But God sent a test in my life, and I found out I was not nearly as sold out to God as I had thought. I had to deepen my commitment, but at the moment of testing, I was not as committed as I had led myself to believe.

And the point is that we will never realize how truly committed we are to Him until we are tested, until we are tried in the crucible of pressure and stress. So, God tests us in order that we may find out our level of commitment—and hopefully move forward and onward and deeper from there.

The second reason that God will test us is that *He wants to reveal to us His faithfulness when we are going through the test.*

The only way in the world you will ever discover how faithful God is to you is for Him to put you in a "stretch" position, a position where, if God does not come through, you are going to fall flat on your face. None of us likes that position. But that is precisely how you and I discover how faithful God is.

The testing times are rough, tedious, nerve-wracking, but they are times when we learn of God's never-ending faithfulness. There are scores of promises in the Word which speak of His faithfulness.

There is another truth which leaps out at us. *In the*

testing of our commitment, God always teaches us new truth. Going through my spiritual diary, and looking at the times God has tested me, I notice that every time I was tested, there was a new insight or truth Charles Stanley learned. God revealed a new aspect about Himself—His ways, His plans, His purposes, His method of operating in my life.

God's testing is never for the purpose of His learning about our commitment. Testing is always for our own benefit and edification. God not only wants us to discover truth about Himself and ourselves, *but God always wants us to grow.* We grow by understanding more and more about God's workings in us and those around us.

One of the best approaches to instructing your children is to teach them about these Old Testament heroes of the faith. Help your boys and girls to read and study the lives of Abraham, Isaac, Jacob, Daniel, David, Joseph, Joshua, Sarah, Hannah, Rebekah, Ruth, and others. If they do not read yet, read the stories to them from the Bible. Also use Scripture-based Bible story books in the language small children can understand. Show your boys and girls how God has worked and is working. The most exciting stories are in the Word of God.

The more you and I understand the ways of God, the more we will recognize how to respond when the testing comes. We learn that God operates by certain principles which are good and beneficial for us. Now, you cannot box and label the Lord, but you can become conversant with the basic principles of His dealings with us.

So, what happens? He wants us to grow in our understanding of how He operates; *He wants us to grow in our devotion to Him.* We love Him even more when we are "stretched," tried, and tested; and He wraps us in His arms of love, envelops us in Himself, overshadows us with His loving care, carries us triumphantly and victoriously through that time of testing, thus deepening our dedication to Him.

Another principle of His purposes is: *He wants us to grow in our faith.* One of my favorite hymns is "Trust and Obey," because I believe you could sum up God's purpose for your life in those two priceless words—*trust* and *obey.* When you learn to trust Him explicitly and implicitly, you will obey Him. If you are obeying Him, it is because you are trusting Him. The more you obey Him, the more you trust Him. The more you trust Him, the more you obey Him. That is a marvelous cycle for the believer who wants his commitment to deepen and grow.

God always *has a definite purpose for driving us to the very edge in our Christian lives,* and we pray, "Dear Lord, I can't take any more." But we can because He is with us.

Now we have dealt with His *purpose* for testing us. Now let us consider the *promise* that God gives us when we are tested in our commitment. There are two lovely promises here. The first main word is *control,* and the second is *companionship.*

Whenever God tests your commitment and mine, there are at least two promises He makes: *He has promised to control the testing,* and *He has promised His companionship in that testing.*

In 1 Corinthians 10:13 there is a promise you ought to carry with you at all times:

> There hath no temptation [trial, testing, difficulty] taken you but such as is common to man: but God is faithful, who will not suffer [allow, let, permit] you to be tempted [tested, tried] above that ye are able [to stand is implied]; but will with the temptation [testing] also make a way to escape that ye may be able to bear it.

God always puts a limitation on His trial, so He knows exactly what we can endure. He is aware of how you can be tested. God is so good in that He does not reveal when we are first saved all the tests and trials we are going to endure. If He did, most of us would cry out, "Lord, take me now. Forget the rest of my life. There's not going to be any way I can live through all of this."

I love that old song, "God Leads His Dear Children Along." He does that. There is a test here, and a test there, but He has promised never to put on us more than we can bear.

He also promises His companionship in that He will never leave us or forsake us. I need Him all the time, but I especially need a definite sense of His presence when I am on the brink and asking, "O God, what's going to happen now?"

And you continue communing with Him and praying, "Lord, the main thing I need to know is You are with me—You will bring me through this. Lord, I need to know You are going with me."

When God is with you in the up's and down's, you can handle it far better. Do you understand why people become alcoholics, dope addicts, and libertines, wrecking their lives? They have no comfort and no Comforter. They are without God. Booze, pills, reefers, and lasciviousness are all substitutes for the deep-down satisfaction they would receive if only they had Jesus as their Counselor. When their testing comes, they turn in every direction but heavenward.

One of my favorite verses is Joshua 1:9:

> Have not I commanded thee? Be strong and of a good courage; be not afraid, neither be thou dismayed: for the Lord thy God is with thee whithersoever thou goest.

Why and how can we make it through the testings? Because He is with us. He "knows the pain we feel," goes the old song. Another one expresses it, "If Jesus goes with me, I'll go anywhere." What a tremendous truth! Yes, when I am tested He has the testing under control—and He is my Companion. He is walking with me every step. Sometimes you may almost panic and ask, "Lord, where are You in this? Lord, I don't see You. I don't feel you. I haven't heard from you recently." But He is there all the time.

Not always by my emotions, but by His truth, I recognize that He is closer than my heartbeat, my breath, the processes going on in my body. He is nearer than my oxygen and my white and red corpuscles. I believe He is so intimate because He has become your life and mine.

After His *purpose* and His *promise,* there is the *perplexity of it all.*

Look at Abraham. Remember that he was one hundred years old when Isaac, the child of promise, was born. God had promised to bless all the nations of the earth through Abraham's posterity, and that his descendants would be plentiful like the sands of the sea shore. Believe me, that is plentiful in profusion. But He tested Abraham by calling for his most precious treasure, Isaac. "Take now thy son, thine only son Isaac, whom thou lovest, and get thee into the land of Moriah; and offer him there for a burnt offering upon one of the mountains which I will tell of" (22:2).

Abraham had waited and waited for that son. He had for all practical purposes given up hope—so had Sarah.

In Genesis 22:3 it is interesting to note that Abraham rose up early, as though he were rushing to perform the will of God. I do not think I would have slept all night. Even if I had not I would have stayed in my tent a long time, and I probably would have walked the floor all night, would have walked a long distance and protested to the Lord, "You know I'm going to do what You say, but I just can't understand this request. Surely there is something amiss, Lord. After all, You promised that my seed would multiply. Kill my only son, the son You promised? You can't be serious. This doesn't make sense. What about Your promises? What about the Promised Land? What about my descendants as the sands of the sea shore and the stars of the sky? What about all the nations of the earth that were going to be blessed by my descendants? Now, You have given him to me for such a short time, and You want me to kill him? Why?"

That is probably what I would have said to God, but Abraham did not. There was not one questioning note about him. He did as He was commanded without a mumbling word.

Think on four words. Number one is: *unreasonable.* Oftentimes when God tests our commitment to Him, the first thought we have is: *It's unreasonable.* It is hard for us to put ourselves in Abraham's sandals. Surely God would never tell you to kill your son, to sacrifice a life. He would never insist that you do anything that violates His law and His will and His principles and His purposes.

God was *testing* Abraham, the man He had chosen to carry on the message of the Almighty. Of course, God dealt with Abraham through the one person in life he cherished above all else, with the exception of God. "Take now, thy son, . . . and offer him there for a burnt offering."

When we are tested—if we recognize the situation as a test—we ask, "Why? This seems so unreasonable. Irrational. It makes no sense. Why are You putting me through this?" You have heard this scores of times at funeral homes and at gravesides, "Why did God do this to me? Why did He take my husband, my wife, my baby?" And the person always seems to be oblivious to the fact that multitudes of people die every day around the world. It is as though no one else has ever gone through trials and tribulations; no one else has ever undergone the death of a loved one.

When you ask all of the questions, for a time you may hear nothing but dead silence. What counts most of all is not handfuls of answers—but the help which comes from knowing He is with you. You may feel that the test is *unreasonable.*

Second, you may feel it is *untimely.* Not only "Why, Lord?" but "Why, *now,* Lord? Why at this particular time? Why when it looks as if everything is going well? Why, Lord, when I thought all was copacetic? Now it looks as if the world is caving in. Look, I've tried to be obedient, to serve You. My life, my career, my future seem to be coming apart at the seams. Why, now, God?"

Abraham could have asked all of those questions, but he did not. Have you asked the Lord those deep questions?

There is another word—*unfair.* We may feel, "It's unfair, God. I don't know which way to turn. I'm between a rock and a hard place. The unsaved don't seem to go through as much as I do."

We cannot ascertain what Abraham thought. Did he

ask God, "Why are You doing this to me? Why are you making this request? I am following You. I'll give up my herds, my wealth, my servants, but to ask me to give up my son is more than I can stand. God, ask me to relinquish anything else, and I will do it immediately."

I have noticed that God is not impressed with our cries of unreasonable, untimely, and unfair. That does not move God at all.

The last "un" is *unbearable*. God has never promised to answer all of our why's. He has promised to keep our testing under control, and likewise He has given us the assurance of his companionship to walk with us through the testing.

Indeed the entire situation may be perplexing at times. No reasonable answer. Very untimely. Seemingly unfair and unjust. And almost unbearable. Can you conceive of standing over your child with a knife? That dear child for whom you had prayed, that child you have diapered and fed and nurtured and cared for? That child with whom you have hunted and fished and played and cooked? That child you taught to pray, to play baseball or football? And God asks you to give up that child.

No. Not one of us could do that without protesting, "God, this couldn't be Your real wish. Surely this couldn't be from You." There are many voices which are not His voice. Any word, any voice, any message you receive, regardless of who delivers it, that tells you to violate even one principle of God's Holy Word is straight from hell, from the devil, from Satan himself. It is Satan's lie, and do not listen to it.

Many people today alibi by explaining, "God told me to do it." Sometimes they are committing all kinds of evil and crime, and blaming it on God. God never intended ultimately for Abraham to kill his son. God never would have allowed that. But He used the test to vindicate Abraham's unswerving faith. God knew what He was doing so Abraham would discover to what degree he was committed to Jehovah, Elohim, YHWH, Adonai. He wanted Abraham to know. God already knew.

The fourth word is *painful.* Yes, it is. My, how we have hurt, how we have suffered, how we have agonized. Probably the most painful hurt is emotional, deep within the heart where it stings and bites and gnaws worse than physical hurt. Like Jesus prayed in the Garden of Gethsemane, "My soul is exceeding sorrowful, even unto death."

Now here is what we struggle with most of all—that soul-crushing emotional pain. We are committed, or think we are committed, and we hurt internally; many times we can share it with no one but Jesus.

Then we often ask, "What makes it hurt on the inside when we are trying so hard to please God?" Now this is why we hurt . . .

It is not because God is being unkind to us. The hurt is at this point—when the sincere, committed Christian is tested and he wants to do the will of God with all of his being, but he feels too frail and weak to follow through on his commitment.

It is like putting your ear to the railroad track. Did you ever do that as a child or teenager? You listened for the train and heard it singing in the track, even though it was miles away. You recognize that somewhere along the track the test is coming. You want to stop that train of testing, but you cannot. Now God is not going to run you over, but He will let you hurt for your own growth and edification.

So, we hurt because we so desperately want to obey and serve God—but we are weak. As Jesus put it to his followers, "the spirit is indeed willing, but the flesh is weak." The struggle is there, the hurt, the pain, the anxiety. It was in Abraham's heart, but the Scripture never indicates that he questioned or even thought as we think when the testing crushes us. I cannot help but think that Abraham struggled. He was after all human. Yes, and even Jesus struggled in the Garden of Gethsemane as those great sweat drops of blood gushed from the pores of His skin.

Abraham was unequivocally committed to God, but he was also a daddy. And a daddy would have a difficult time killing his son, except in extreme circumstances.

Somehow I believe that Abraham thought within his heart, *Even if I take his life, the Sovereign God (YHWH, Elohim), on the basis of his unconditional promise to me, will have to resurrect him from off of that altar!*

That is why he indicated to his young servants, "Wait here, and *we're* coming back." Yet, even if he knew God were going to resurrect his son, can you envision shoving a dagger into your child's heart?

Then let us consider the *progressiveness* of it. God moves us onward and upward in our commitment to Him. Notice the growth and progression in the life of Abraham. Nothing leads us to believe that Abraham was anything but a pagan before God caught him up and called him out of Ur of the Chaldees. Abraham did not know who this God was until God led him along, introduced Himself to him. Think of the spiritual development in the life of Abraham, and it had come down to this ultimate crisis—sacrifice your son. Leaving Ur and going to an unknown land was a snap in comparison to this test.

There was an immeasurable amount of water under the bridge between "leave your family" and "offer your son." And God will mete out our trials by degrees and times. I have heard people remark, "Now, Lord, I'll pray for You to send me trials." You need not pray like that. Rest assured that He will send them! And He will send them for your own good. For the moment you will not be able to understand those trials.

In his divine economy God realizes that we must grow and stretch. As we do, our faith increases. Our commitment deepens and expands. As that happens we "grow in grace and in the knowledge of our Lord and Saviour Jesus Christ" (see 2 Pet. 3:18). Then we become more useful and valuable to His kingdom.

Guess why certain people feel so purposeless and

useless. It is because back there God tested their commitment, and they flunked. They never left first base. They are in the past still asking questions and trudging on a treadmill. Many of those became angry and bitter. They blamed their test on people, not being willing to accept the test as coming from God. They remain in the kindergarten of commitment when today they ought to be in graduate school!

When you answer "no" to God, He tends to draw the line. He whispers deep in your heart, "You let Me down. You were not willing to pass through the test and accept it as from Me, even though I assured you of My presence and that I would stick with you."

You may have stopped growing. You cannot be committed and stop growing. Neither can you be rebellious toward God. God is sending you through a process of progression.

If only you and I could see life from *God's perspective.* He makes no mistakes. God will not countenance our giving orders and directions to Him. Many of us simply cannot stand the responsibility of commitment. When we commit ourselves, God begins to make all kinds of requests. Study the Word. Have a steady prayer life filled with meditation and praise. Witness. Make witnessing your life-style. Minister in the name of Jesus. Volunteer for work in the church. It goes on and on, and all you do will involve pleasing God and serving Him, even if it lacks recognition in this life and is unheralded and unsung.

To live a life of commitment, it will mean not being happy with the status quo; it will imply giving up a laissez faire policy toward the things of God. God will continue to raise the level of your commitment as you follow Him. And if you protest, "I can't keep up; I want to stay right here," He will reply, "Nothing doing. There are no plateaus on the spiritual plane." He will want you to move onward and upward to "higher ground."

Sometimes, when we balk, God has to give us a shove, a push. When He does, it is an expression of His amazing grace and love to us. He does not want us to stay where we are, because staying where we are means stagnation.

Have your children talked with you about what is involved in growing up, after you have explained the pressures of paying your bills? "Good gracious, after listening to you talk about all those bills—the mortgage, the car payment, food, clothes, insurance, utilities—and how tough it is to make a living, I think I'll stay a teenager! I don't think I want to grow up if I have to face all of that." Then what do you say to them? "OK, stay thirteen years old. That's all right. Don't grow up. That'll be fine." Oh, no, you lay it on the line: "You're gonna have to grow up and face the same things that your mother and I encounter."

Yes, certain aspects of life are tough, but here is what I have discovered. The tougher and the more strenuous the stretch, the greater the growth, the understanding, and the internal development of your spiritual life.

Notice another key word—*performance.* All of us are going to perform in one manner or another after being tested—and even while we are being tested.

We will respond according to our understanding of who God is, who we are, to whom we belong, and why we are here. When I begin to grapple with those four ideas, it will affect my response to God's testing.

Then I want you to receive this: your response and my response are going to be based on our genuine love and devotion to Christ. Christ knows you are going to pass through a period of agonizing when you begin to realize you are being tested. He will listen to your arguments, your rationalizations, and your feeble protests for a time. He knows that when you pass through the fog, the haze, the maze of all your attitudes, you will pray, "Lord, I don't understand it, but I accept it. I'm trusting You. I'm going on with You!"

But in all of this testing from God, do not think Satan is inactive. Satan will try to whisper, "Ah hah, just look at you now, committed Christian, child of God, follower of Jesus Christ." Now you are not going to let the devil faze you, are you? Because when you are in the heat of the testing time, you will look back and think, *in the center of the will of a sovereign God is where I am, and God promised to be my Controller and Companion in all of this.*

Every test is also God's method of sifting out our own stubborn will from His "good and acceptable and perfect will" (see Rom. 12:2). Many times it is our will versus

His. Through testing we move in the direction of complete yieldedness to Him, finally realizing that our will is no good until it coincides perfectly with His.

Then you can honestly pray to the Lord, "Lord, I am in the center of Your will, right where You want me to be—nothing wavering. Even if all hell breaks loose against me, I can thankfully recall the struggle which brought me to this place of total surrender."

God wants to work into your life the same qualities He incorporated into Abraham's.

Like him, we now have two options at this point. We can trust and obey God, or we can become fearful and attempt to escape—to flee. It is always the summum bonum to obey God and then leave the consequences of our obedience to Him. Without exception it is always the best policy. Obey Him. Even if you have to close your eyes and leap out into seeming darkness, trust Him. Adhere to Him. In the final analysis you will always come out a winner.

Finally, record this word in your mind—but more than that on the tables of your heart. *Profit.* It always profits us when we are tested and we obey Him. Now do not immediately think in terms of material or monetary profit, even though God could honor your obedience in that area. But, to me, the greatest profit is the reward of having our commitment tested in this inexplicable, overwhelming, bubbling, abundant, overflowing joy of simply sensing, "I obeyed God! I did what He wanted me to do! I performed His will for my life!"

There is nothing in all of the Christian life more satisfying than that. It is spectacular. The absolute God of the universe is in your life, offering you a challenge concerning your partnership with Him—and you have passed through Mount Moriah and the fiery furnace and the den of lions, as it were, and you have remained faithful and loyal to Him—and you have followed through on your definite decision to serve and obey Him. What matters most of all, not even counting the other manifold spiritual blessings, is to know, "Dear God, I have obeyed You, and I understand You are pleased with me."

The more intimately you live with Him, the more sensitive you become about grieving Him. That is true in marriage. If you love your spouse deeply, you will not want to offend him/her for long, if at all. Hurting your mate hurts you, if there is a depth of love and commitment to each other.

And the more intimately you live with Christ, the less you can disobey Him. He lives in you (see Gal. 2:20). By hurting Him you are wounding yourself because He is an integral spiritual part of you.

The greatest lesson you can teach your children is, "My child, obey God at all cost." And God will honor you and your children. You cannot obey God without being blessed. Rejoice with Abraham in Genesis 22:15-18:

> And the angel of the Lord called unto Abraham out of heaven the second time, and said, By myself have I

sworn, saith the Lord, for because thou hast done this thing, and hast not withheld thy son, thine only son; That in blessing will I bless thee, and in multiplying I will multiply thy seed as the stars of the heaven, and as the sand which is upon the sea shore; and thy seed shall possess the gate of his enemies; and in thy seed shall all the nations of the earth be blessed; because thou hast obeyed my voice.

Can you imagine the overwhelming joy which must have swelled up in Abraham? The ram caught in the thicket (v. 13) and this pronouncement constitute two of the highest points of Abraham's life.

If only I could convey to you how crucial it is that you obey God. Hang in there with Jesus through the testing times. If you obey Him, I will make this guarantee: through your intimate relationship with Him, you will emerge with a new sense of overwhelming assurance and confidence about your own life.

When you can walk away from the fierce test, realizing you may have been bloodied, bruised, and broken, you can have the exhilaration of realizing, "I have obeyed God!" There is no substitute for that peace within your heart!

C H A P T E R 6

Commitment:

THE REWARDS OF OBEDIENCE

2 Kings 5

Make no mistake about it. God always rewards commitment and obedience to Him. Study your Bible from Genesis to Revelation, and you will discover that principle in every Book.

God always rewards obedience, but there is a companion truth to that—our failure to obey God leads to pain and suffering eventually.

Neither the reward nor the suffering are always immediately recognizable in one's life, but eventually they are going to surface—either the joy of our rewards, or the pain of our suffering.

None of us should be obedient just because we want to be rewarded. We will be rewarded, but that should not be our main motivation. There are three primary reasons you and I should be motivated to obey God.

One of them is: *He is God.* Because He is God, and He is the Sovereign of the universe, He deserves to be obeyed.

Second, *He is a wise God and requires only what is*

best for us. His wisdom dictates that we always do what is beneficial for us in the light of His truth.

Third, *motivation ought to be from our devotion and love to Him.*

Now, are you doing what God wants you to do? What are you doing about His call to commitment? What are you doing about your marriage, your vocation, your family, your schooling, your relationships, your finances, your giving, the entire spectrum of your life?

There are three answers to the above.

- Yes, I am doing what God wants and is telling me to do.

- No, I am not doing what God wants me to do.

- Yes, I am doing what God is telling me to do, but I am not doing all that He is telling me to do. I am being partially obedient to Him. (That is one of the devil's favorite tricks.)

As I explained in the chapter on "Resistance to Commitment," partial obedience is actually disobedience. There is no such thing as "sort of" obeying God.

Second Kings 5 presents a perfect example of a person struggling with obedience. The final result of our central character's obedience was deliverance and joy. This passage applies to every one of us in every facet of life.

Let me give you the Bible background for five basic principles I want to share. If you apply these to your life, you will be motivated to commitment and obedience. If you incorporate them into your being, you will miss loads of heartaches, countless mistakes, and tons of torture here. The Scripture opens:

> Now Naaman, captain of the host of the king of Syria, was a great man with his master, and honourable, because by him the Lord had given deliverance unto Syria: he was also a mighty man in valour, but he was a leper (v. 1).

Naaman was a brave and highly respected military man. God had allowed him success in military campaigns, and he had delivered Syria. But over all of his prestige and position, there was hanging a dark cloud—leprosy.

To this day leprosy is considered a horrid disease, even though cases are rare, and there is treatment to keep it under control. Leprosy unabated is horrendously destructive. The disease deadens the nerve endings, so lepers continually hurt themselves since they have no pain, or not much. In addition, the disease sloughs off the appendages of the body, the fingers, the toes, the nose, the ears, the lips. In the worst cases recorded in medical history, the victim is hardly recognizable as a human being.

Somehow Naaman had continued to function as the captain of the host. The situation was different from Israel. If he had been in Israel, they would have segregated and ostracized him, but in Syria he was allowed to serve the king. Still, he had a disease which was incurable and becoming worse.

Verse 2 records that there was a little maid from Israel who waited on Naaman's wife. The Syrians had captured her on one of their raids into Israel. In verse 3 the maid suggested to her mistress, "Would God my Lord were with the prophet that is in Samaria! for he would recover him of his leprosy." She was speaking about Elisha, the successor to Elijah the Tishbite.

The maid was winsome and convincing to Naaman's wife. When Naaman came home, his wife gave him the jubilant news.

The king of Syria insisted that Naaman contact the prophet right away. "Go to, go, and I will send a letter unto the king of Israel. And he departed, and took with him ten talents of silver, and six thousand pieces of gold, and ten changes of raiment" (v. 5).

If my arithmetic is correct, he carried a million dollars with him. The king, it is plain to see, thought highly of Naaman. When the letter was delivered to the king of Israel, he was fit to be tied. The king of Israel misunderstood the letter, thinking perhaps that he was expected to do the healing (v. 7). The king was tearing his clothes in perplexity, worrying himself sick over the letter.

In verse 8 Elisha heard of the situation. He sent a message to the king: "Wherefore hast thou rent thy clothes? let him now come to me, and he shall know there is a prophet in Israel." "Send Naaman, and he will see the power of God," is what he meant.

Next, Naaman came with his horses and chariot, and stood at the front door of Elisha's house. Mind you, he was the captain of the Syrian host. Elisha sent a messenger or servant out to greet him. Elisha himself did not show.

The messenger delivered Naaman's prescription:

> Go and wash in Jordan seven times, and thy flesh shall come again to thee, and thou shalt be clean (v. 10).

Naaman, to put it mildly, was sorely angry. Naaman had his own preconceived notions of how the prophet of God would perform. "Behold, I thought, He will surely come out to me, and stand, and call on the name of the Lord his God, and strike his hand over the place, and recover the leper [namely himself]" (v. 11).

Then he began to rave and rant in a huff.

> Are not Abana and Pharpar, rivers of Damascus, better than all the waters of Israel? may I not wash in them, and be clean? So he turned and went away in a rage (v. 12).

Naaman was mad as a wet hen! He wanted his healing, but he wanted it according to his own prescription rather than God's. I can almost hear him, "How can you make such a suggestion. You wouldn't even dignify my presence by coming out to meet me. You sent nothing but a hired servant. And then You insulted my pride and intelligence by telling me to wash seven times in the

Jordan River, that dirty little Israelite stream, that polluted body of water. Why, the waters of Damascus are so clear and fresh in comparison to all the bodies of water in Israel. Hummppfff!"

Verse 13 shows the calm thinking of his servants. They called him father. "The prophet had bid thee do some great thing, wouldest thou not have done it? how much rather then, when he saith to thee, Wash, and be clean?"

What a simple request! Elisha was not asking him to round up the Eight Wonders of the World, to fly, or to jump off a thousand-foot cliff and not be hurt. It was a basic direction. What could he lose?

As Paul Harvey would narrate it, you know "the rest of the story." Naaman did precisely as he was told. He dipped himself seven times in the muddy Jordan, and his flesh came again like unto the flesh of a little child, and he was clean" (v. 14).

Against that backdrop I give you five principles that will be rewarding in every instance where you apply them.

First of all, *our needs are oftentimes God's opportunities.*

What was the most pressing need in Naaman's life? Not prestige. Not prosperity. Not position. Not prominence. It was to find healing for a dread disease that could have slowly killed him, wearing away his body in the process. It mattered not that he had money, servants, family, prestige, the favor of the king, and popularity as a military hero. He needed a cure for his leprosy!

Sometimes God may send a need. I am not claiming God sent the leprosy upon Naaman, but He certainly allowed it to happen. He allowed the leprosy in order for Him to perform a dramatic work that not only influenced him but the nation of Syria. Sometimes God allows a need to enter your life, and He could create that need.

What did God want to teach Naaman? He wanted to teach him that the God of Israel was and is the true God, that the evidence of His sovereignty was seen in His cure of a disease no human being could possibly heal. Further, He wanted to teach him to trust in the God of Israel. And He wanted to teach him how important it is to be obedient to God—to place his trust and obedience in God—and to demonstrate that God would reward obedience.

For us today God creates the need; then He challenges us to stretch our faith and to be obedient to Him. As we obey Him in the church, He rewards us as a body. He rewards us individually and as families. Obedience leads to rewards.

First of all, *the need indicates that God wants to teach us something.* Secondly, *obedience may often require what seems to be impractical and unreasonable.*

To sum up, Naaman was incensed because Elisha would not even come out to meet him. And plunging into the Jordan River seven times seemed so ridiculous and messy. There was nothing rational about it. Many people today object to New Testament baptism by immersion. They think it is unnecessary and impractical. They think it looks silly. They do not want to get wet. They will mess up their hair. Naaman used the same approach.

More than likely Naaman might have been thinking, *Wait a minute! If my dipping in the Jordan River will heal me of my leprosy, how come all the lepers from Israel aren't swimming and filling up that river for the purpose of being healed?*

This is the reason—because God did not tell anybody else to wash in the Jordan River seven times. If you look around to see what other people are doing, and choose to be obedient on the basis of what they are doing, you will surely end up disobeying God. You and I must be obedient on the basis of what God tells *us* to do. He does not always have the same instructions for each and every one of us. I can be obedient only for me, not for another person—and I cannot base my obedience on another person or persons.

If God instructs you to do something impractical from a human standpoint, do it. He may ask you to leave your house or apartment at an odd time, and He may have an unsaved person waiting for you. Do you remember Philip being instructed, "Arise, and go toward the south unto the way that goeth down from Jerusalem unto Gaza, which is desert"? (Acts 8:26). Verses 27 through 39 tell of Philip's obedience and the salvation and baptism of the Ethiopian eunuch who was sitting in his chariot out in the middle of that hot desert. Now suppose Philip had argued and questioned and put up all kinds of excuses. The gospel might not have gone to Ethiopia when it did.

Your obedience keeps the door ajar for blessing after blessing. God is going to honor your faithfulness to Him.

When you are obedient in one area, God reveals another area in which He will bless you—until you will cry, "My cup runneth over!" You cannot outgive God, and you cannot outbless Him.

Most strategic in your relationship to Him is the satisfaction of being obedient. When you come down to it, that is reward enough in itself—the light of Jesus' smile, His "Well done, thou good and faithful servant."

Will there ever be any joy in your life, any genuine freedom from selfish bondage until you can declare with all your heart, "Almighty God can be trusted to keep His everlasting Word, every single word of it"?

As long as you have doubts about that, you will never have freedom in the Spirit. Naaman at first responded as you and I are prone to do. We ask, "How practical? How reasonable? How convenient?"

Most of us have never scratched the surface concerning giving to God's causes. Why? Because we have so little faith we are not willing to step out on the promises of God and believe that He is going to care for us on nine-tenths rather than ten-tenths. We have trouble committing to God. Why? Because it is not practical or reasonable or convenient, so we think.

Suppose Naaman had not gone to the Jordan River, or suppose he had given up and plunged in only five or six times. He would have died a leper.

A third thought I want to convey is: *failure to obey God may cost us the very thing we desire most.*

What was the grandest desire of Naaman's heart? Healing of his leprosy, of course. To be cured, to give his wife a clean man, to give his children a healthy father, to stand before the king as an honorable and cleansed warrior. For a man looking toward a horrid death, it was a consuming desire—"I want healing."

In the beginning he was furious and thought the remedy was preposterous. He had three problems. Number one was *pride.* "Me, the captain of the Syrian host, and you won't even come out to see me. What an insult!"

The second was his *anger.* He had the scenario all worked out in his mind. Check out verse 11 again. "Why, surely Elisha was going to come out here and stand before me. And he was going to call on the name of his God, and strike his hand over the place, and heal me right there on the spot." But it did not work like that, and it aroused his ire. Verse 11: "But Naaman was wroth." Verse 12: "So he turned and went away in a rage." He had a nasty temper when he failed to get what he wanted the way he wanted it when he wanted it.

And third was his *unbelief.* At first he did not believe that in obeying the prophet of God, the Lord would cure him of his leprosy. Nothing has changed since then.

Nearly all of us have two or all three of those bugaboos.

Pride rears its ugly head. God asks us to make a commitment, and we explain, "Now, look, Lord, surely I don't have to do that. What will people think? Can't I just sit back here and make my commitment? Why do I have to respond and walk forward?" Or "I'll do some of that, but not all. Lord, isn't part of the apple better than no apple at all? Besides, that'll look stupid, strange, funny to people."

Instead of being overwhelmed by our needs, we ought to be saying, "Hallelujah! What's God going to teach us now? What's going to be His beneficial result from all this?"

We can only imagine how Naaman acted going to the river. He may have mumbled and complained every hoofbeat there. He may have felt sheer humiliation before his retainers. He may have talked to himself, *You dummy, this is the craziest thing you've ever done: listening to that prophet from Samaria. You need to have your head examined!* From time to time he may have sheepishly glanced toward his servants.

He came to the river, and embarrassment set in. Even though he was probably bearded, and his skin was perhaps disfigured and discolored from the leprosy, I imagine he managed a bright-red blush. He probably dipped his toes in first, tentatively, queasily, like we do when we think the water is too cold. And he may have scooped his hands into that muddy water. Tarpon Springs it was not. And he may have growled in his throat. So, he may have held his nose as he went down the first time. One time. Nothing happened. He may have commented, "See there. I told you. Nothing's going to happen." Twice. Nothing. "What did I tell you?" Three times. "The same old disease." Four times. "Nothing's changed." Five times. Six times. "My, my, just as I thought all along." Perhaps his concerned servants yelled, "Master Naaman, seven times, not six. You're already there. It's not going to hurt. Just one more time. You'll never know if you don't try." So he gritted his teeth and plunged in the seventh time.

You know the story. He was miraculously healed. Many of you ladies would like to have a skin treatment like that. He did not come up with the skin of a middle-aged man—all rough, scarred, weatherbeaten. His skin, the Word of God states, was like that of a baby's. Smooth. Lovely to touch. Not a wrinkle, not a blemish.

And I imagine Naaman and his retinue had a foot-stomping, back-slapping time. The difference was: they were praising the Lord God of Israel, not some dumb Syrian fertility idol.

> And he [Naaman] returned to the man of God, he and all his company, and came, and stood before him: and he said, Behold, now I know that there is no God in all the earth, but in Israel: now therefore, I pray thee, take a blessing of thy servant (v. 15).

What had God told you to do? Have you done it? Or have you done only part? Not six times, but seven. Not partly but totally.

Obedience is doing what God says, when God says it, how he says to do it.

You do not need to understand. Why the Jordan River? Why seven times? Why didn't Elisha come out to greet Naaman? Why? As the poet wrote: "Ours is not to reason why, ours is but to do or die." God calls us to be obedient. That means leaving many of our why's behind us. Why is OK for a small child. That is how he learns. "Why, why, why?" Many times parents have to answer, "Because I said so," "Because we said so," "Because that's right," "Because if you don't, we'll have to spank you." But you are supposed to have grown in the Lord. Quit asking why so much. Instead ask "What?" "What do you want me to do, Lord?"

Obedience is the pathway to blessing. Malachi 3:10 in principle applies to all of our lives, not only to money and material possessions.

> Bring ye all the tithes into the storehouse, that there may be meat in mine house, and prove me now herewith, saith the Lord of hosts, if I will not open you the windows of heaven, and pour you out a blessing, that there shall not be room enough to receive it.

Whatever you give (whether money, property, time, talent, energy, abilities, but most of all you) carries with it that promise. Does God have you? There is no end to the blessings He has in store for You if only you will commit yourself to Him and follow Him in obedience.

Many are the times I have had to deal with my own

heart while sitting on the platform waiting to preach. I have talked with myself, *Listen, you can't preach that sermon until you've handled this between you and the Lord. Do it now.* And I have done that on the platform.

Sometimes you may have claimed, "I have no attachments." If you are a Christian, you are eternally attached. You are scheduled for God, booked for Him. We are to live unattached to the things of this world, but attached to Jesus—yes, as an extension of Him and His Will.

The most important consideration is not what you have or do not have, but *what has you?* What are you captured by? What are you captivated with? What are you dominated and controlled by? "Where your treasure is, there will be your heart also," declared our Lord. When you become obedient, He will free you from enslaving habits. He will present you victory over the devil.

There is a fourth principle. *Right counsel always encourages obedience to God.* Naaman was blessed with assistants who cared. They helped cool him down when he was about to storm back to Syria without even going to the Jordan. They advised him, "Please try it. It can't hurt. You're here now. Dip in the Jordan."

Watch out for the counsel you seek. Young people, leave the pot smokers, cocaine sniffers, and pill poppers alone, except to witness to them. You have no business asking ungodly kids what to do. Seek out friends you meet in church and who serve the Lord Jesus and live separated lives. Adults, beware of those who are "worldly wise," who believe there is nothing wrong with compromise. All of you, never listen to a person who seems to stifle your direction toward the Lord and your performance of His will. Steer clear of those who say, "Now, listen, don't go too far. Maybe God's not telling you to serve Him. Hey, weigh this carefully. Don't get carried away. Why, who ever heard of such a thing?" And it is a disgrace that many professing Christian parents talk to their kids like that when they come in and exclaim, "Hey, Mom, hey, Dad, I feel like God is calling me to full-time Christian service. Yeah, I believe that God wants me to preach" or "God wants me to be a missionary."

It is marvelous when husbands and wives are on the same wavelength of commitment and obedience. It is tragic when a couple is pulling in different directions. If your mate is out of fellowship with the Lord, live as closely to Christ as possible. Be kind and loving. Set an acceptable example. Express your love. Pray for your mate. But remember that you cannot depend on a backslidden mate's counsel in spiritual areas.

Further, I want to challenge you to tell God: "Whatever you have placed in my possession is Yours, Lord. It belongs to You."

One last principle is: *the rewards of your obedience will strengthen and encourage your faith and the faith of others.*

Naaman was obedient—finally—and he influenced

his entire army and the nation of Syria, and it was initiated by a little Israelite girl who served Naaman's wife. That chain of influence is phenomenal. One girl—Naaman's wife—Naaman—Naaman's household—Naaman's servants—the king—the army—the entire nation of Syria. He was converted to the Lord of Israel.

Please allow me this experience from our church, the First Baptist Church of Atlanta. We bought a piece of property, and in the negotiations the people who owned the property said, "We don't want the money now. We only want it a month at a time because of our tax situation. So, you cannot pay us cash. This is the only way we will sell it." We needed the property, so we agreed. We negotiated with them for the interest rate, and the primary party agreed, "That appears acceptable to me."

When the time rolled around for us to sign the contract and settle everything, they upped the interest one percent. One percent does not sound large, but over a period of time it would be a tremendous amount of money. We could not do without the property. The buy was still a good deal, so we went ahead with it, knowing it was God's plan for us to have the property.

Three months passed by, and I received a phone call. Someone wanted to make an appointment with me. The party introduced themselves when they came in for the appointment. The person said, "I want to tell you what happened to me. I'm not a Baptist. When we were negotiating about the building you purchased from us, I said to my partner, 'That church has plenty of money, so let's raise the interest one percent. They can afford it.' "

Of course, that was their decision, and we lived with it. The person continued, "Last week I woke up at 2 o'clock in the morning, and Jesus was standing at the foot of my bed. Jesus said to me, 'That's not THEIR church; that's MY CHURCH. You raised the interest on ME, not on them.' "

That person was so frightened the daughter was called on, and the two of them figured up what that one percent amounted to on the calculator. That person pulled out a check and gave it to me with these words: "I have got to be obedient to God. The interest rate you all offered was right. I was being selfish when I had it raised." And that person handed me a check for the difference! It is amazing how God works in Naaman's life and in that person's life and in your life and mine.

Whether or not Jesus stands at the foot of my bed, He is in my heart, even closer than the foot of the bed. And I am going to obey Him. The rewards of obedience are multitudinous.

Will you pray now that God may have first place in your life, "that in all things he might have the preeminence"? (see Col. 1:18).

Lord, we humble ourselves before You, reaffirming our obedience to You whatever the cost may be. We open our hands, gripping nothing, stripping ourselves of everything of the world that may attach itself to us—and everything to which we are attached in order that we may be totally free—that Your power may flow through each one of us, God, that we may walk uprightly, obediently before You. This is our commitment and our prayer in Jesus' magnificent name. Amen!

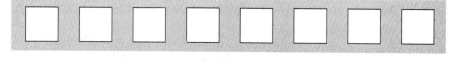

Epilogue:

IS JESUS CHRIST YOUR LORD?

Crown Him with many crowns, The Lamb upon
    His throne;
Hark! how the heavenly anthem drowns
All music but its own!
Awake, my soul, and sing
Of Him who died for thee;
And hail Him as thy matchless King
Thro' all eternity.

            —Matthew Bridges

    Fairest Lord Jesus, Ruler of all nature . . .

"Take up thy cross and follow Me,"
I heard my Master say;
"I gave my life to ransom thee,
Surrender your all today."

. . . .

My heart, my life, my all I bring
To Christ who loves me so;
He is my Master, Lord, and King,
Wherever He leads I'll go.

            —B. B. McKinney

In the final analysis, it boils down to one question for you and me as Christians: Is Jesus Christ in truth the Lord of your life? Of my life?

A central principle of a conquering Christianity is: "Jesus Christ is Lord!" Christians through the ages have suffered, bled, and died, spurred onward by that affirmation—He is Lord!

As I have explained throughout the foregoing pages, we cannot be committed, obedient, and surrendered to Him until we acknowledge Him as Master, Lord, and King.

There are many names for Jesus in the Word of God. He is the Messiah, Shiloh, the Water of Life, the Bread of Life, the Son of God, the Son of Man, the Redeemer, the Rock, the Rose of Sharon, the Vine, the Lily of the Valley, the Chief Cornerstone, the Bright and Morning Star, the Fairest of Ten Thousand, the Savior . . . and the Lord. That is a partial list. Lord seems to stand out. From a concordance I counted every time Lord and Savior are employed. The word *Lord* appears 7,633 times, whereas Savior occurs only thirty-six times! In the New Testament, Lord is used 736 times, almost always referring to the Lord Jesus Christ.

For God to major on that word, it must be exceedingly important in His divine economy and plan. The only word utilized more than *Lord* in designation to Jesus Christ is *Jesus*.

Let this mind be in you, which was also in Christ Jesus: Who, being in the form of God, thought it not robbery to be equal with God: But made himself of no reputation, and took upon him the form of a servant, and was made in the likeness of men: And being found in fashion as a man, he humbled himself, and became obedient unto death, even the death of the cross. Wherefore God also hath highly exalted him, and given him a name which is above every name: That at the name of Jesus every knee should bow, of things in heaven, and things in earth, and things under the earth; And that every tongue should confess that Jesus Christ is Lord, to the glory of God the Father (Phil. 2:5-11).

One day *every* knee shall bow and every tongue shall confess that Jesus Christ is Lord. Yet, I want to pose this question: Have you done that now? *Then* it will be too late. Have you weighed the Bible-based questions asked virtually on every page of this book?

Are you committed to Him, obedient to Him, sold out to Him, turned over to Him, following Him, seeking His guidance, doing His will, acting on His commands, engaging in His ministry, doing His bidding with all your being? Is Jesus Christ Number One in your entire life? Does He have preeminence? Is He first? Is He supreme? Have you fully acknowledged His rightful claim on you? Is He Master, Lord, and King? Does He reign on the throne of your heart?

Mary gave excellent advice to the servants at the wedding feast in Cana of Galilee, "Whatsoever he saith unto you, do it" (John 2:5). In other words, "Whatever he tells you, follow it down to the minutest detail." Those servants moved into action and prepared themselves and the wedding guests for Jesus' first public miracle.

There are two words translated *lord* in the New Testament. One of them is *despotas,* from which we receive our modern word despot, which has come to mean a cruel taskmaster or tyrant. Today the word refers to a master who "lords it over" his servants or slaves for his own selfish end. This word is never capped as a title.

The other word, employed as a title for Jesus, is *kurios. Kurios* (Lord) carries with it the idea of headship of a husband and father over his family—a kind, caring, loving, tender, protective relationship. This word for Lord means a lordship which is benevolent and beneficent, for the good of those under one's leadership or lordship. When the Bible refers to Jesus as Lord, it is never as a despot. His Lordship is always for our own good, never for a selfish end.

Several years ago I was in the hospital. Sometimes I feel one of the main purposes of hospitals is to afford us places to collect our wits and think. I began thinking, *Is Jesus really my Lord?* Occasionally I have given myself a Lordship inventory. In that hospital bed I asked myself, *What is really involved in my being committed and obedient to the Lord Jesus?*

If you have read the preceding chapters, give yourself a spiritual inventory.

We recognized Him as Lord, but there is a difference between Jesus being THE LORD and being *my* LORD. Is He *your* Lord? We as Christians have recognized Him as Lord, but what is the difference? Jesus Christ is Lord, regardless, "Every kindred, every tribe on this terrestrial ball" will one day "crown Him Lord of all!" He is Lord whether or not we accept His Lordship over us.

First, there is the *revelation* of His Lordship. He is Lord. He is Master. He is King.

Second, there is the realm of His Lordship. His Lordship is manifestly indicated throughout Scripture.

> In whom we have redemption through his blood, even the forgiveness of sins: . . . (Col. 1:14).

Paul establishes the *redemption* we have through His shed blood. In Him there is forgiveness and cleansing. "What can wash away my sin? Nothing but the blood of Jesus."

> Who is the image of the invisible God, the firstborn of every creature: For by him were all things created, that are in heaven, and that are in earth, visible and invisible, whether they be thrones, or dominions, or principalities, or powers: all things were created by him and for him (Col. 1:15-16).

Jesus Christ is not merely an agent of creation—He is the Creator. He is the Lord of creation. John in his Gospel opened with: "In the beginning was the Word, and the Word was with God, and the Word was God. The same was in the beginning with God. All things were made by him, and without him was not any thing made that was made" (John 1:1-3).

In Colossians 1:18, Paul proclaims that Jesus is the

head of the church. His Lordship includes the church, the company of the redeemed which has received the redemption earlier spoken of in verse 14.

Revelation 17:14 makes the declaration:

> For he is Lord of lords, and King of kings: and they that are with him are called, and chosen, and faithful.

The conclusion of Colossians 1:18 emphasizes that "in all things he might have the preeminence"—he must have first place, not only in the church, but in "all things."

His realm of Lordship includes the church, the church which is often asleep and drowsy, the church which is often not watching and waiting, the church which does not appear to be implementing Jesus' command to "occupy until I come." It is high time that we accepted Him as the head, the Lord of the church.

Revelation 19 records His mighty return, when He comes back as a Bridegroom for His Bride, the born-again saints of God. "And he hath on his vesture and on his thigh a name written, KING OF KINGS, AND LORD OF LORDS." In the original and in a number of translations His designation was in caps.

Jesus is Lord over every facet of life. Romans 14:11 expresses that truth:

> For it is written, As I live, saith the Lord, every knee shall bow to me, and every tongue shall confess to God.

It is difficult for a lost and dying world to realize that

whether or not it acknowledges Him now, it will later. All of us have heard the words of the commercial, "You can pay me now or you can pay me later."

The third thought under Lordship is the *recognition we give Him as Lord*. There is no such commodity as part acknowledgment of His Lordship. We must recognize Him as Lord and mean it with every fiber of our being, following through on the dictates of that Lordship.

Most of us are willing to think of Him as the God of creation. "Beautiful Saviour, Lord of creation." We give all kinds of lip service and formal affirmation of His Lordship, but this is the crux of the matter: *In what areas of your life is He Lord? What is actually involved in His being your Lord? How can I ascertain if He is Lord of my life?* Not merely because I claim He is, not merely because I sing it or speak it.

After all is said and done, how do you know He is truly Lord of your life? If you cannot answer that question, if you cannot determine where you stand, I feel the foregoing chapters have not fulfilled their intended purpose.

All through the Scriptures the Word emphatically states that Jesus Christ is Lord. What criteria are there by which you can gauge your adherence to His Lordship? You may reply, "Well, I'll just compare myself to Jesus, match myself up to Him." You will never make it. You also will not make it with a *random* reading of the Bible.

While in that hospital bed I prayed to the Lord, "Lord, show me something that is practical, something that is brief enough for me to memorize and learn, something to check against my daily life and experience to discover if Jesus Christ is the Lord of my life on a practical basis."

There are eight principles I leave with you.

1. Jesus Christ is my Lord when I obey the initial promptings of the Holy Spirit without hesitation or argument. In other words, "What He says to you, do it."

2. Jesus Christ is my Lord when I am committed to fulfilling His will for my life before I even know what He will require of me.

3. Jesus Christ is my Lord when I am available to serve Him without regard to time, space, or circumstances.

4. Jesus Christ is my Lord when I recognize His ownership of my total life and all of my possessions—and submit to that ownership.

5. Jesus Christ is my Lord when pleasing Him exceeds my desire to please others. The Psalmist prayed, "I delight to do thy will, O God."

6. Jesus Christ is my Lord when I look to Him as the source of all my needs and desires. God will work out His providential provisions in our lives. He may do that through His divine intervention or He may employ others to fulfil our needs and desires.

7. Jesus Christ is my Lord when I am turning my difficulties and my failures into opportunities for spiritual growth. This is one radiantly marvelous

weakness, even as He did the snoozing of the disciples in dark Gethsemane. He was disappointed in them, but he was cognizant of their frailty, saying: "The spirit indeed is willing, but the flesh is weak" (Matt. 26:40c).

Once I thought if a pastor dared to admit difficulty, weakness, or failure, such an admission was terrible. After all, how dare one of God's men confess to vulnerability? But I looked at the tremendous personalities of the Bible—and, with the exception of the Lord Jesus, "they blew it." I also saw how God turned their imperfections and weaknesses into opportunities. So I began to relate to their imperfections—not their strong points.

As believers we must be willing to isolate the difficulties in our lives and look at them from God's perspective, drawing spiritual precepts from them. If we are not willing to do that, He is not fully Lord of our lives. If we are not accepting these impediments for growth, then we are saying to God, "God, what you are allowing to happen is bad. Why did you do that? Lord, I think what you've allowed to happen is horrid."

Either we will resist or we will accept adversity as having a positive purpose from His standpoint. Acceptance will conform us to the image of God's dear Son.

We are the Lord's. We belong to Him. He has the right to send whatever He wishes. In life we are responsible for our actions. In death we are accountable for how we have spent our lives.

Finally . . .

8. Jesus Christ is my Lord when to know Him intimately becomes the obsession of my life. There must be total commitment, obedience, and availability for His use. Ephesians 6:5 is an admonition to slaves—bondservants, those who were owned by a master. There is a sense in which the verse is intended for us today, even though we are not chattel. We do *belong* to the Lord Jesus *if* He is our Lord. That verse insists, "Servants (the word for bondslaves), be obedient to them that are your masters according to the flesh, with fear and trembling, in singleness of your heart, as unto Christ." In other words, serve others on behalf of Christ. Jesus taught us, "Inasmuch as ye have done it unto one of the least of these my brethren, ye have done it unto me" (Matt. 25:40).

Will you embrace those eight Biblical principles I have shared with you? You will discover that, as God unleashes these factors in your life, you will be busy serving others in Christ's name. God gives us what He does only in order for us to give it away for Him.

Is Jesus Lord of your life as a Person? In honesty you may have to answer, "No, Lord, You're not." You may have to confess that you are not committed and obedient.

dient.

How does He become Lord? How do we transform casual Christianity into compassionate, concerned Christianity? How can we exemplify commitment? How can we walk in obedience?

Under the leadership of the Holy Spirit and the nurture of God's Word, review the eight criteria of His Lordship in our lives. Start confessing this moment. You may have to admit shortcomings with all eight.

It is not enough to call Him Lord. He is King of kings and Lord of lords, whether or not you are committed and obedient to Him.

He will never be satisfied with being called His divine titles until you and I can testify from the heart, "Jesus Christ is *my* Lord." And neither will you.

May the words of Isaac Watts's old hymn, "Am I a Soldier of the Cross?" haunt us in our comfort and convenience, our casual Christianity:

Must I be carried to the skies
On flow'ry beds of ease,
While others fought to win the prize,
And sailed through bloody seas?

. . . .

Sure I must fight if I would reign;
Increase my courage, Lord;
I'll bear the toil, endure the pain,
Supported by Thy Word.

CONFRONTING

Casual
CHRISTIANITY

STUDY GUIDE

The study guide is designed to help you study, understand and apply the principles written in this book. There are interactive questions and activities for each chapter. It is suggested that you answer the study questions chapter by chapter. Take the time to reflect on what you have just read. Do not skip any of the study questions and activities. Many of the activities require you to interact with both the material and with God through prayer and reflective thinking.

INTRODUCTION

1. In your own words, define apathy.

    _____

    _____

2. Tell about a time of apathy in your own life.

    _____

    _____

3. Dr. Stanley uses the Biblical account of Gethsemane found in Matthew 26:36–46 as an example of apathy. Read Matthew 26:36–46 and answer the following:

    A) What did Jesus tell the three disciples to do?

        _____

        _____

    B) When Jesus returned from praying what were the three doing?

        _____

        _____

    C) How did Jesus respond?

        _____

        _____

    D) Did the three obey the second time?

        _____

E) How does Dr. Stanley use this Bible account to teach about apathy?

_____

_____

F) What do you have in common with the disciples in Gethsemane?

_____

_____

4. What do you see that indicates the Christian church today has a propensity toward a casual, comfort-seeking brand of Christianity?

_____

_____

5. What two antidotes for apathy and complacency will Dr. Stanley present in this book?

_____

and_____

* Ask God to show you any areas of complacency in your personal Christianity. Begin a list of complacency areas. Make giving these to God a part of your daily prayer time; be honest with God as you give your apathy to Him.

CHAPTER ONE—COMMITTED

1. In your opinion why are so many churches partially empty on Sunday morning?

    _____

    _____

2. On page 23, what answer does Dr. Stanley give for the problems of churches today?
    Write out his exact words:

    _____

    _____

    _____

3. Explain the difference between making a decision about Jesus and being committed to Him.

    _____

    _____

    _____

4. In 1 Peter 4:19, "Wherefore, let them that suffer according to the will of God commit their souls before him in well doing as unto a faithful creator," circle the word commit.

What does commit mean in this verse?

_____

_____

5. Complete this statement: According to the Word of God, to make a commitment means to:

    _____

    _____

    _____

6. List some synonyms for this kind of commitment:

    _____

    _____

    _____

7. Answer this question presented by Dr. Stanley, "Since you were saved, has there been a time in your life when you consciously committed all of your life to Jesus Christ—without hesitation, without reservation, without bargaining with God?"

    _____ Yes
    _____ No

If your answer is yes, tell about that time when you committed your life to Jesus.

_____

_____

8. Compare partial commitment and degrees of commitment.

   Partial commitment: _____

   _____

   _____

   Degrees of commitment: _____

   _____

   _____

9. Following the airplane illustration used by Dr. Stanley on page 30, how would you describe your commitment to Jesus right now? Check the appropriate box:

   ❑ Sitting on the runway   ❑ Flying
   ❑ Revving my engines   ❑ Taking off
   ❑ Crashing to ground

10. Why did you pick your answer in question nine?

   _____

   _____

   _____

11. What are some of the results that can occur if you refuse to obey God?

   _____

   _____

   _____

12. Rewrite in your own words the central truth of commitment that Paul gives in 1 Corinthians 6:19.

   _____

   _____

13. In light of Romans 12:1-2, define commitment.

   _____

   _____

   _____

14. Have you committed your life to Jesus with no strings attached?

   _____ Yes
   _____ No

15. What two forces work against our commitment to Jesus?

   _____

   and_____

16. How does the lure of the world stand in the way of your commitment to Jesus?

_____

_____

_____

17. How does the love of convenience and comfort stand in the way of your commitment to Jesus?

_____

_____

_____

18. What should be your motivation for committing your life to Jesus?

_____

_____

_____

19. Is it time for you to affirm your commitment to Jesus?

_____

_____

_____

20.   Are you willing to be totally available to God in service and ministry?

_____

_____

_____

*   Write a prayer of commitment to Jesus. If you are not ready to make this commitment, write a prayer asking God to work in your life to show you what stands in your way to make a total commitment to Jesus. Read this prayer out loud to Jesus.

CHAPTER TWO
THE CALL TO COMMITMENT

1. Complete this statement: Less than total surrender is:

   _____

   _____

2. In Exodus 2:4, Moses took an important step in answering God's call to commitment. What did he do?

   _____

   _____

3. List any things in your life from which you need "to turn aside" in order to listen to God:

   _____

   _____

   _____

4. Dr. Stanley gives one pressing reason why the Christians of America are not making a strong impact on society. What is his reason?

   _____

   _____

   _____

5. What changes do you see happening in your local Christian community if more believers were totally committed to Jesus?

   _____

   _____

6. Identify the four questions that must be answered and understood before anyone can be totally committed to Jesus:

   1) _____

   2) _____

   3) _____

   4) _____

   Note: This next section of questions and activities will deal with the above four questions.

7. WHO IS THIS GOD?

   Read the following verses from Exodus 3 and circle the words or phrases that identify who God is:

   Verse 6: Moreover he said, I am the God of thy father, the God of Abraham, the God of Isaac, and the God of Jacob. And Moses hid his face, for he was afraid to look upon God.

Verse 7: And the Lord said, I have surely seen the affliction of my people which are in Egypt, and have heard their cry by reason of their taskmasters; for I know their sorrows.

Verse 14: And God said unto Moses, I AM THAT I AM; and he said, Thus shall thou say unto the children of Israel, I AM hath sent me unto you.

Verse 15: And God said moreover unto Moses, Thus shalt thou say unto the children of Israel, The Lord God of your fathers, the God of Abraham, the God of Isaac, and the God of Jacob, hath sent me unto you; this is my name for ever, and this is my memorial unto all generations.

Verse 16: Go, and gather the elders of Israel together, and say unto them, The Lord God of your father, the God of Abraham, of Isaac, and of Jacob, appeared unto me, saying, I have surely visited you, and seen that which is done to you in Egypt.

Answer these questions:

A) Why was it important for Moses to know who God was?

_____

_____

B) Why it is important for you to know who God is?

_____

_____

C) Imagine that you are Moses. Explain to God's people why they can trust you to be their leader.

_____

_____

8. WHO AM I ?

A) Read the third paragraph on page 52. Compile a list of who you are as one who has put his trust in Jesus:

_____   _____

_____   _____

_____   _____

B) Read this excerpt and circle all of the action words that describe you, the believer.

"You have been forgiven of your sin; you have been redeemed by the grace of God; you have been justified, declared righteous, and God now looks upon you as though you had never sinned. You have been pardoned from your sins by His blood. You have been reconciled to God through His Son, Jesus Christ. You have been sanctified, and are being sanctified (set apart) unto God and for Him. You have been gloried as a child of God, a child of the King."

C)   Now explain why you have forfeited your "rights."

_____

_____

_____

9.   TO WHOM DO I BELONG?

A)   What are the excuses Moses gave God in Exodus 4:10?

_____

_____

B)   Identify any excuses you have used to explain to God why you could not undertake an assignment:

_____

_____

C) How did God demonstrate His power to Moses?

_____

_____

D) How has God demonstrated His power to you?

_____

_____

E) Dr. Stanley states, "If you are the purchased possession of the Lord Jesus Christ, you do not belong to yourself." Make a list of any areas in your life where you have drawn boundaries and have not given possession to Jesus.

_____

_____

10. WHY AM I HERE?

A) What was the task to which God called Moses?

_____

_____

_____

B) Review the special providential acts of God
    in Moses' life:

    1) _____

    2) _____

    3) _____

    4) _____

    5) _____

C) Begin a list of the special providential acts of
    God in your own life:

    1) _____

    2) _____

    3) _____

    4) _____

    5) _____

D) How does God use "dry spells" in a
    person's life?

    _____

E) Draw lines matching the Scriptures on the
    left with the purposes for a believer's life on
    the right.

Matthew 5:16	Glorify God with our spirits
1 Peter 2:12	Glorify God with our voice
Romans 15:6	Glorify God with our body
1 Corinthians 6:19–20	Glorify God with our works

F) Complete the following statements:

I glorify God with my voice by:

_____

I glorify God with my body by:

_____

I glorify God in my spirit by:

_____

These works of mine glorify God:

_____

* Ask God to show you what you need to understand and apply in the material found in this chapter.

11. Summarize the most meaningful insight you learned from this chapter.

_____

_____

_____

12. What does God want you to do in response to this insight?

_____

_____

_____

CHAPTER THREE
MOTIVATION FOR COMMITMENT

1. Define motivation.

    _____

    _____

2. Read Daniel 1:8 and paraphrase "Daniel pur-
    posed in his heart."

    _____

    _____

3. Identify the five motivating factors for Daniel's
    commitment:

    1) _____

    2) _____

    3) _____

    4) _____

    5) _____

4. Write a summary statement that describes devo-
    tion.

    _____

    _____

5. Describe how your devotion to Christ works like an anchor.

    _____

    _____

    _____

    _____

6. Complete this statement: Daniel received clear direction from _____ through _____.

7. Where can Christian's go for God's clear direction?

    _____

    _____

8. How does "busyness" block clear direction from the Lord in your life?

    _____

    _____

    _____

9. *Read this prayer of commitment out loud: "Lord God, I am committed to obeying You, regardless of the circumstances."*

10. Try to picture what God might do in and through your life if you follow through on the above commitment. Describe what could happen.

_____

_____

_____

_____

11. How does the following quote make you feel about commitment? "When you make a leap of faith, you are always going down in the palm of the sovereign hand of God."

_____

_____

_____

_____

12. What does king Darius' response in Daniel 6:16 tell you about Daniel's witness?

_____

_____

_____

_____

13. "Daniel was unafraid of the consequences." Compare yourself to Daniel in standing up against a crowd by completing this diagram.

DANIEL   BOTH OF US   ME

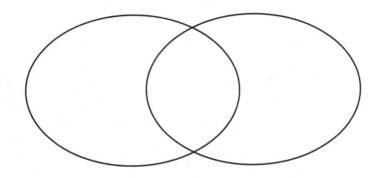

14. Mark each of the following statements YES or NO.

_____ I am willing to confront people with the truth of Jesus Christ.

_____ I hesitate to witness for Christ.

_____ I have made a commitment to obey my Lord Jesus whatever the consequences.

* Ask God to show you what you need to understand and apply from this chapter.

15. Summarize the most meaningful insight you learned from this chapter.

_____

_____

_____

_____

16. What does God want you to do in response to this insight?

_____

_____

_____

_____

CHAPTER FOUR
RESISTANCE TO COMMITMENT

1. In what direction did Jonah go when he ran from the presence of the Lord? _____

2. "There was a mighty tempest in the sea." Describe any tempest in your life which is or was caused by you not surrendering your will to God.

    _____

    _____

    _____

3   List the reasons we resist commitment to the Lord:

    1) _____

    2) _____

    3) _____

4. What are some common fears that cause us to resist commitment to God?

    _____

    _____

    Circle the fear that holds you back.

5. Read Jonah 4:1-2. Identify Jonah's root problem.

   _____

   _____

6. The second reason why we fail to follow through on our commitments to God is based on:

   _____

   _____

7. Name any selfish "gourd vines" which are keeping you from totally committing to God.

   _____

   _____

8. Circle TRUE or FALSE. God seeks those who know they are inadequate outside of His power.

9. Identify the four ways we show resistance to God:

   1) _____

   2) _____

   3) _____

   4) _____

   Put a red star by the way you use the most to resist God.

10. Circle TRUE or FALSE. Partial obedience is still disobedience to God.

11. Which is the correct step to take when God tells you to do something? Check one.

    _____ Consult with friends.

    _____ Get on your knees and pray.

12. What are two results from denying God's will in your life?

    1) _____

    2) _____

 * Ask God to show you what you need to understand and apply from the material you've just read.

13. Summarize the most meaningful insight you learned from this chapter.

    _____

    _____

    _____

14. What does God want you to do in response to this insight?

    _____

    _____

    _____

CHAPTER FIVE
COMMITMENT ON TRIAL

1. Abraham is known as a man of faith and commitment. Read Genesis 22:1 and circle the phrase that shows Abraham's obedient, committed response.

    "And it came to pass after these things that God did tempt (test) Abraham and said unto him, Abraham: and he said, Behold, here I am."

2. What is Abraham's response in Genesis 22:11?

    _____

3. Do you want to be totally committed to the Lord Jesus Christ?

    _____ Yes

    _____ No

    Which of the following statements describe a deep commitment? Check the appropriate statements.

    _____ Acknowledging Jesus' final authority in my life's decisions.

    _____ Being totally available to God's directions.

    _____ Being totally submissive to God's call.

_____ Giving no arguments or rationalizations to God's call.

_____ Giving up a laissez-faire policy toward the things of God.

4. Go back to question 1 and reread Genesis 22:1. What did God do to Abraham?

_____

_____

_____

5. Identify the two reasons why God tests our commitment to Him.

1) _____

2) _____

6. Fill in the blanks to review some purposes of God's testing.

A) In the testing of our commitment, God always teaches us _____

B) Testing is always for our own _____ _____ and _____.

C) God not only wants us to discover truth about _____ and

_____,but God always
wants us to _____.

7. How do we grow?

_____

_____

8. Share a time of growth in your life that God
brought about through testing.

_____

_____

_____

9. Dr. Stanley presents some basic principles that
God uses. List these purpose-based principles.

1) _____

2) _____

3) _____

10. In 1 Corinthians 10:13 God gives us two
promises about testing, what are they?

1) _____

2) _____

11. How do these promises help you deal with testing?

_____

_____

_____

12. Read Joshua 1:9. Write out God's promise.

_____

_____

13. Identify the five words that often describe our feelings toward testing.

_____, _____, _____,

_____, _____.

14. How does God's promise in Joshua 1:9 help you deal with the above negative responses to testing?

_____

_____

15. Explain the progressive nature of God's testing.

_____

_____

_____

16. Our performance is affected by our understanding of these four questions:

   1) _____

   2) _____

   3) _____

   4) _____

17. How does Satan get involved in our testing?

   _____

   _____

   _____

18. What are the two options of response to God's testing?

   _____

   or _____

19. What is the profit we receive when we are tested and we obey God?

   _____

   _____

* Ask God to show you what you need to understand and apply from this material.

20. Summarize the most meaningful insight you learned from this chapter.

   _____

   _____

   _____

21. What does God want you to do in response to this insight?

   _____

   _____

   _____

CHAPTER SIX—COMMITMENT: THE REWARDS OF OBEDIENCE

1. Fill in the blanks to summarize the truth about obedience.

    God always _____

    obedience, but our _____

    to obey God lead to _____

    and _____.

2. List the three primary reasons to be motivated to obey God.

    1) _____

    2) _____

    3) _____

    Did you list rewards as a motivation for obedience?

    _____ Yes

    _____ No

    Rewards will happen but should not be a main motivation.

    _____ Agree

    _____ Disagree

3. Rate your commitment in the following areas by choosing one of these responses, and writing it in each of the boxes below:

A) Yes, I am doing what God wants and is telling me to do.

B) No, I am not doing what God wants me to do.

C) Yes, I am doing what God is telling me to do, but I am not doing all that He is telling me to do. I am being partially obedient to Him.

Areas:

☐ marriage ☐ family

☐ finances ☐ schooling

☐ vocation ☐ church

☐ relationships ☐ giving

☐ ministry ☐ witnessing

☐ spiritual growth

4. Put yourself in the place of Naaman and explain your struggle with obedience.

_____

_____

_____

5.   What do you have in common with Naaman?

     _____

     _____

6.   Complete the five principles regarding obedience and rewards.

     1)   Our needs are often _____

        _____

     2)   Obedience may require what seems to be

        _____

     3)   Failure to obey God may _____

        _____

     4)   Right counsel always _____

        _____

     5)   The rewards of your obedience will be

        _____

7.   Name the three problems which caused Naaman to resist obedience:

     1) _____

     2) _____

     3) _____

8. Complete this sentence: Obedience is

   _____

9. Instead of asking "why, Lord?" ask

   _____

10. What is God's principle presented in Malachi 3:10?

   _____

   _____

   * *Ask God to show you what you need to understand and apply from this material.*

11. Summarize the most meaningful insight you learned in this chapter.

   _____

   _____

12. What does God want you to do in response to this insight?

   _____

   _____

EPILOGUE:
IS JESUS CHRIST YOUR LORD?

1. List the evidences in your life that show that Jesus is truly your Lord.

   _____

   _____

2. Define Jesus' title as Lord (Kurios).

   _____

   _____

3 Name the three "R's" that define the difference between Jesus as The Lord and Jesus as the Lord of your life.

   R _____

   R _____

   R _____

4. Summarize the eight principles to use as a check against your daily life to see practically if Jesus is the Lord of your life.

   1) Jesus Christ is my Lord when

   _____

   _____

2)   Jesus Christ is my Lord when

_____

_____

3)   Jesus Christ is my Lord when

_____

_____

4)   Jesus Christ is my Lord when

_____

_____

5)   Jesus Christ is my Lord when

_____

_____

6)   Jesus Christ is my Lord when

_____

_____

7)   Jesus Christ is my Lord when

_____

_____

8)   Jesus Christ is my Lord when

_____

_____

5. Go back to the last study question for chapters 2-6 and list the responses that God led you to make:

    _____

    _____

    _____

    _____

    Do you still feel that these are responses that God wants you to follow?

    _____ Yes

    _____ No

6. *Write your own prayer of commitment to the Lordship of Christ in your life.*

    _____

    _____

    _____

    _____

Date _____

*Signature*_____

Now, give this prayer to the Lord Jesus Christ.